Silence, Solitude, Simplicity

A Hermit's Love Affair with a Noisy, Crowded, and Complicated World

SISTER JEREMY HALL, OSB

Foreword by
Kathleen Norris

LITURGICAL PRESS
Collegeville, Minnesota

www.litpress.org

Excerpts from *Sayings of the Desert Fathers: The Alphabetical Collection,* trans. by Benedicta Ward, SLG, Cistercian Studies 59 (Kalamazoo, MI: Cistercian Publications, 1975): World Rights in English by permission of Benedicta Ward, SLG.

Excerpts from *The Desert Fathers,* trans. by Helen Waddell (London: Constable & Co Ltd, 1987 [1936]): Rights in English for the United Kingdom by permission of Constable & Robinson Ltd, London; and World Rights in English exclusive of the United Kingdom by permission of The University of Michigan Press, Ann Arbor.

Unless otherwise stated, the Scripture quotations are from the *New Revised Standard Version Bible,* © 1989 by the Division of Christian Education of the National Council of Churches of Christ in the U.S.A. Used with permission. All rights reserved.

Cover design by David Manahan, OSB. Photo courtesy of iStockphoto.com and © Maartje van Caspel. Photo of the author by Fran Hoefgen, OSB.

Typeset by Monica Weide

1   2   3   4   5   6   7   8   9

Library of Congress Cataloging-in-Publication Data

Hall, Jeremy, 1918–
    Silence, solitude, simplicity : a hermit's love affair with a noisy, crowded, and complicated world / Sister Jeremy Hall ; foreword by Kathleen Norris.
        p.   cm.
    Includes bibliographical references.
    ISBN-13: 978-0-8146-3185-0
    1. Benedictines—Spiritual life.   2. Spiritual life—Catholic Church.   I. Title.
    BX3003.H35   2007
    248.8'943—dc22

                                                                    2006102425

Contents

PART III: GOD'S QUESTIONS

Editors' Preface

"*T*HE MORE I PRACTICE, THE LUCKIER I GET." Sister Jeremy Hall, OSB, might say about her Benedictine life what Gary Player said about his golf game.

Her book is the fruit of decades of practice, decades that have behind them the millennium and a half that daughters and sons of Saint Benedict and his twin sister Saint Scholastica have practiced seeking God after a monastic manner of life. And it goes back even farther. Sister Jeremy has drunk deep at the wells of wisdom, laced with humor, of those ascetics who flocked to the deserts of Egypt and Syria in the two centuries before Benedict.

But there is nothing musty, cobwebbed, nostalgic in these pages. Sister Jeremy, in her late 80s, is totally alert to the world around her and within us. She is allergic to sentimentality. Because she has spent so much time in silence—she lived as a hermit for twenty years—she is especially attentive to words and how like a chameleon they can be. Her antennae are sensitive to anything phony.

Sister Jeremy, born in 1918, joined Saint Benedict's Monastery in St. Joseph, Minnesota, in 1940. But she had come to the community earlier, in 1936, when she enrolled at the College of Saint Benedict. So Sister Jeremy has been part of this women's monastic community for almost half its one-hundred-fifty-year history, and the publication of this book in 2007 is a fitting accompaniment to Saint Benedict's Monastery's sesquicentennial.

This book is in three parts, which—as Sister Jeremy says about monastic ideals and practices—are all of a piece, woven together but identifiable separately. At first glance, her teaching might appear directed at other monastic persons, but what she knows is something millions of people in recent years have come to understand. The monastic way is not forsaking the world, but for the sake of the world, and Benedictine wisdom is fundamental human wisdom. "We all need God," she says in her first sentence, and readers of all sorts will find here a warm and practical address to that need.

Part I, "A Benedictine Way to God," has components and emphases that will be familiar to anyone even slightly acquainted with monastic spirituality; but there is a freshness, a lucidity to Sister Jeremy's account of Benedictinism that could come only from a long lifetime spent in thoughtful commitment. She never forgets that at the end of the Rule (73:9) Benedict says that even if you have done everything in it, the most you can claim is to have made a good beginning. She recounts not an accomplishment but an attempt, provides not a blueprint of a destination but the itinerary of a journey.

And it is nobody's journey but hers—which makes it, paradoxically, something from which everyone can learn. "I did" is much more effective teaching than "one might" or "you should." Even when Sister Jeremy quotes someone else, you know she has made the source her own, the other voice has given expression to her experience.

Part II, "Desert Spirituality," is the special fruit of Sister Jeremy's years as a hermit. All that time alone made her an acute interpreter—in current jargon we might call her a channel—for the insights of those ancient folk whose pared-down life stripped veils from their eyes so they saw themselves, the world, and God with unnerving clarity. Silence, solitude, and simplicity—unavoidable in the desert—are keys to authentic speech, true community, and abundant life. The desert, after all, blooms.

Part III, "God's Questions," is a demonstration of one of a Benedictine's most characteristic activities, *lectio divina*, "sacred reading," a way of meditating on texts, especially the Bible, in which the text burrows into the heart. Sister Jeremy takes us through a series of questions that Scripture poses to us—Where are you? What are you looking for? Who do you say that I am? Will you turn back and live? Where is your faith? Can you drink this cup? Do you love me?—and shows how a monastic's answers put her, not on a pedestal or behind a wall, but right in the thick of things with all of us.

Now and then in this book you will encounter pages with a lightly shaded background. The words—some of them poems—are reminiscences of Sister Jeremy's early years that she wrote when living as a hermit, from her mid-60s to her mid-80s. She called this brief journal "Grace Notes," and we have included the extracts because we believe that is precisely what they are.

It has been our privilege and honor to edit Sister Jeremy's words, written at different times and for various occasions, but glowing in every sentence with her graceful and witty and hospitable spirit. She is a boon companion, an inspired teacher, a trustworthy guide, a fool for Christ, one of God's great ones. In Sister Jeremy's company you will glimpse, as we have, the Christian life as W. H. Auden said it could be: "You will see rare beasts, and have unique adventures."

Patrick Henry
Kathleen Kalinowski, OSB
Stefanie Weisgram, OSB

Foreword

*I*T IS SAID THAT PILGRIMS VISITING the ancient monasteries of the Egyptian desert could easily pick out the venerable Anthony in a crowd of monks, for this man who was renowned as a hermit literally glowed with hospitality. His life of prayer in solitude had rendered him visibly open and welcoming to others. This mystery of the monastic life—and it is a true mystery, not merely a paradox—is one that we also encounter in the life and work of Sister Jeremy Hall.

I first had the privilege of meeting Sister Jeremy in the fall of 1990, when she was recommended to me as a spiritual confidant. *But she is a hermit,* I thought: would I not be intruding on her quiet life, making a difficult calling even more difficult? Approaching her with some trepidation I was glad to discover that she was genuinely hospitable and one of the best listeners I have ever known. Sister Jeremy epitomizes one archetype of the monastic life, that of the person who may not have any special education, training, or certification in spiritual direction, yet is sought by a broad variety of people seeking wise counsel. Hildegard of Bingen was such a one, advising popes, princes, and peasants alike. If you are familiar with a monastic community you can probably name the person who is regularly consulted by the abbot or prioress as well as the newest postulant, a young mother from the parish, a teenager or two, and even the neighborhood dogs.

If you are not familiar with monastic life, this book will provide an excellent introduction, for monasticism is but one expression of the human longing for God, and the questions that Sister Jeremy raises about seeking God in both solitude and community are essential ones for anyone, Christian or not, who desires a more balanced and holy life. As a compilation and distillation of years of Jeremy's retreat talks and musings, this volume is replete with gems. Her discovery that gratitude is the flip side of desire, for example, and that neither is sufficient unto itself.

One sign that this book is a fruit of a truly contemplative life is that Sister Jeremy consistently embraces mystery and redefines aspects of human psychology and spirituality in such penetrating and liberating ways. Her insistence that silence reflects a reverence for speech, especially God's word; that humility is properly understood as authenticity; that true prayer unites the mind and heart. If we allow it, this book might seed and plow our souls, helping us to embrace more fully that life to which God is calling us, whatever it may be. We might more readily and effectively, as John Cassian put it in the early fifth century, "work the earth of our hearts."

Another aspect of this book that appeals to me as a Protestant is the richness of scriptural interpretation it offers. It is clear that the biblical word is Sister Jeremy's constant companion and that working its metaphors and narratives into her own story has become as natural for her as breathing. At a time when biblical scholarship is too often left to scholars alone, and the Bible is employed as a bludgeon to denigrate whole classes of people, the refreshment provided in these pages is true nourishment. We are challenged not only to enjoy but to grow.

And when Jeremy reflects on God's questions to biblical characters—Where are you? What are you looking for? Who do you say that I am?—we come to understand that these are questions she has taken to heart as those she must seek to answer for herself, even if it takes a lifetime. And we may wonder if God has asked us these questions as well, but we have responded with a deaf ear.

For those who are tempted to view monastic life as anachronistic or escapist, Sister Jeremy offers the rebuttal of contemplative wisdom, seeing that to live out of compulsions—even that of activism for a good cause—is to acquiesce to violence. We do violence to ourselves and those around us, she asserts, whenever we work obsessively or seek myriad distractions rather than face up to ourselves. We are meant to be free, but are often afraid to claim that freedom. Sister Jeremy names as essential for spiritual health the gratitude, reverence, and trust that are so often lacking in our world and observes that it is in accepting God's love for us that we begin to restore what we have lost.

At a time when so much meaningless diversion passes for entertainment, we need Sister Jeremy to remind us that our lives do have meaning, and that we were created to find it. I find it inspiring that her focus is ever fixed on the purposes and ends of human activity, the "whys" that keep us seeking after truth. We are fortunate indeed that Sister Jeremy has shared with us her life as a stable searcher and hospitable hermit, a life that in her words has taught her that the desert is for the Promised Land as Lent is for Easter, and death is for more life. It is only silence, she insists, that allows God's word to enter and transform us, only solitude that can foster true community, only simplicity of life that will enrich us beyond anything we can imagine. The wealth of spiritual wisdom on these pages is remarkable, yet mundane. This book, as well as the witness of Sister Jeremy's life as a monastic woman, demonstrates what can happen when an ordinary person honestly seeks to embrace the monastic call to what Jean Leclercq so memorably termed the love of learning and the desire for God.

Kathleen Norris
Ash Wednesday, 2007

Part I

A Benedictine Way to God

Chapter 1

Desire:
A Homesickness at Home

E ALL NEED GOD. This is a fundamental human reality. We are radically incomplete and broken within; this is how we experience ourselves. Individuals who have sought a monastic life came to the monastery in desire, open to God's attraction, God's power to draw; but this openness to God's attraction is experienced by millions who know little or nothing of monasticism. Desire is the basis of community itself, as well as of each one's own response to God and to one another in community.

Saint Gregory the Great, pope at the end of the sixth century, the first biographer of Saint Benedict, and probably a monk himself, is called "the Doctor of Desire." He speaks in his homilies of holy desire as a yearning for God that is rooted in human nature itself, a basic orientation to God, whose redeemed image we are. It could be called a homing instinct, eliciting what Chesterton called "a homesickness at home." But like all good things, this desire can fade. Can we renew or reawaken it?

Desire is nourished by Scripture. The whole of the Old Testament is permeated by longing—for wisdom, for Jerusalem, for the temple, for

3

knowledge of the word and the law of God. All these are expressive, ultimately, of a desire for God himself. And they are often couched in terms of hunger and thirst, the basic demands for life itself.

> As a deer longs for flowing streams,
>   so my soul longs for you, O God. (Psalm 42:2)

> For he satisfies the thirsty,
>   and the hungry he fills with good things. (Psalm 107:9)

> Your name and your renown
>   are the soul's desire.
> My soul yearns for you in the night,
>   my spirit within me earnestly seeks you. (Isaiah 26:8-9)

Jeremiah's desire was a force in him greater than the weariness and anguish that prompted him to try to quench it:

> If I say, "I will not mention him,
>   or speak any more in his name,"
> then within me there is something like a burning fire
>   shut up in my bones;
> I am weary with holding it in,
>   and I cannot. (Jeremiah 20:9)

In the New Testament, Luke's Gospel is bracketed by waiting, the expectancy sustained by desire. It begins with Zechariah and Elizabeth in the temple awaiting the Messiah, and ends with the apostles awaiting the Spirit. This is but a sample; so much of the New Testament is desire for communion—both God's desire and ours. And the New Testament ends with desire:

> The Spirit and the bride say, "Come."
> And let everyone who hears say, "Come."
> And let everyone who is thirsty come.
> Let anyone who wishes take the water of life as a gift. (Revelation 22:17)

It was this same desire that motivated the early monks of the fourth and fifth century to go to the deserts and the gorges and the summits—even to live atop pillars for decades! And it was desire that brought the

TANAGER

A forest pentecost:
a tanager
tongues with flame
this burgeoning birch—
a burst of life
and pledge of benison.

—*Grace Notes*

neophytes to the abbas and the ammas (spiritual mothers and fathers) of the desert for a word of life. If the monk's problem was complacency, he might get a dramatic word to reignite desire. "Abba Lot went to see Abba Joseph and said to him, 'Abba, as far as I can I say my little office, I fast a little, I pray and meditate, I live in peace and as far as I can, I purify my thoughts. What else can I do?' Then the old man stood up and stretched out his hands toward heaven. His fingers became like ten lamps of fire and he said to him, 'If you will, you can become all flame.'"

At roughly the same time as the monks in the desert, Gregory of Nyssa, who deeply affected the spirituality of Eastern monasticism and ultimately that of the West as well, wrote a *Life of Moses* that is studded with desire. Speaking of Moses' desire to see God, Gregory writes: "And the bold request which goes up the mountains of desire asks this: to enjoy the beauty not in mirrors and reflections, but face to face." God's response to Moses: "He would not have shown himself to his servant if the sight were such as to bring the desire of the beholder to an end, since the true sight of God consists in this, that the one who looks up to God never ceases in that desire." Gregory concludes: "This truly is the vision of God: never to be satisfied in the desire to see him. But one must always, by looking at what he can see, rekindle his desire to see more." Almost two hundred years later, Gregory's insight received classic expression in the Rule of Saint Benedict.

Saint Benedict's Way to God

Benedict, the father of Western monasticism, makes it clear that monastic life is for people of desire, and that the life is meant to cultivate and deepen desire. In the Prologue (15) he asks with the Psalmist (34:12), "*Is there anyone here who yearns for life and desires to see good days?*" If you are a man or woman of desire and answer "I do!" Benedict says the Lord will direct you. Again in the Prologue he says, "If we wish to dwell in the tent of this kingdom . . . " (22), and "if we wish to reach eternal life . . . " (42).

In chapter 2:35 it is clear that the abbot is himself to be a man of desire, the prioress herself a woman of desire, seeking first the kingdom and trusting that all else will be given. And the leader's role in the community can be said to be a cultivation of desire, adapting to varied personalities in eliciting a deeply personal response from each (2:23-25). This is made even more explicit in chapter 64:19, in the deservedly beloved words that direct the abbot or prioress so to arrange things that "the strong have something to yearn for and the weak nothing to run from."

Among the tools of good works for the monk, Benedict includes yearning "for everlasting life with holy desire" (4:46) and the aspiration to be holy (4:62). Obedience, he implies, ought to be out of desire, not fear (5:14). In the chapter on humility he speaks of desiring to attain heaven (7:5), and in the fourth degree of humility he suggests that strength of desire should overcome difficulties and injustices (7:37-39). Benedict's beautiful phrase in the midst of Lenten austerity strikes a high point in the Rule: to "look forward to holy Easter with joy and spiritual longing" (49:7).

There is much said of desire, not surprisingly, in chapter 58 on receiving new members. Real desire must be demonstrated before applicants are to be accepted. The criteria for acceptance are seeking/desiring God, seeking God's praise, seeking obedience, seeking the truth of humility—and, by implication, seeking the paschal healing alluded to in the Prologue as the fruit of obedience (58:7; Prologue 2). The applicant who "stands firm" in desire is to be received (58:11-14), and manifests that desire by drawing up the document of self-dedication, putting it on the altar, and singing the *Suscipe* ("Receive me, Lord, as you have promised"), the prayer of desire echoed by the whole community (58:19-22).

All the members of the community are to desire what is best for the rest (72:7), and to desire nothing more than Christ (72:11). The whole of that brief chapter on good zeal is a distillation of desire as it is lived and shared in the community that Benedict envisions.

The final chapter opens further vistas for those hastening along the way of desire. Scripture and the Church Fathers kindle desire as they summon and guide monastics along the way (73:2-5)—even beyond "this little rule that we have written for beginners" (73:8). With desire they can set out for loftier summits with the genuine expectation of reaching them (73:9).

For all this emphasis on desire of the monk, it is important to note that Benedict does not neglect to say that the Lord *desires every individual—*

he seeks us. This, surely, is the ground of the hope, confidence, and trust that are so strong in the Rule.

Desire, then, is a deeply monastic virtue: it is deep in Scripture, in the Desert Fathers and Mothers, and in Benedict. When desire is understood in this way, an otherwise preposterous statement of Father Zosima in Dostoevsky's *The Brothers Karamazov* makes perfect sense, and is an observation, not an outburst of pride: "Monks are not a different sort of person, but only such as all persons on earth ought also to be."

Interlacing of Desire and Gratitude

The elder brother in the parable of the prodigal son (Luke 15:11-24) seems to have known nothing of gratitude. Gratitude is the other side, the accompanying gift, of desire. Jesus made a parable of it in the story of the ten lepers, only one of whom, after they followed Jesus' instructions and were healed, bothered to come back to say thank you (Luke 17:11-19). Scripture is full of gratitude. Those who pray the Psalms daily know the interlacing of desire and petition with remembrance and gratitude. Perhaps this linkage is most frequently and most deeply manifest in Paul. "Do not worry about anything, but in everything by prayer and supplication with thanksgiving let your requests be made known to God" (Philippians 4:6). Neither desire nor gratitude is sufficient or whole in itself; each gives rise to the other, nourishes and intensifies it.

It is this mutual influx of desire and gratitude that sets us actively and persistently and progressively to seek God—initiating and gradually accomplishing the graced return to the Father that preoccupied Benedict. But the search is in the light of faith, which is experienced so often as darkness. There is that awesome sentence in Genesis 15:12 when Abram had prepared the sacrifice of the covenant: "As the sun was going down, a deep sleep fell upon Abram, and a deep and terrifying darkness descended upon him." Gregory of Nyssa says that "the manifestation of God to the great Moses began with light; afterwards God spoke to him in the cloud; next when Moses became more exalted and perfect he saw God in the darkness." Moses learned that whoever desires to behold God sees him in following him, seeing God's back while shadowed by God's hand.

"The contemplation of God's face," says Gregory, "is the unending journey accomplished by following directly behind the Word." And since the desire for this limitless good of seeking the face of God, returning to our Father, is itself limitless, there is no limit to the seeking.

For Job, too, it was a seeking in the darkness of faith:

> If I go forward, he is not there;
>   or backward, I cannot perceive him;
> on the left he hides, and I cannot behold him;
>   I turn to the right, but I cannot see him.

But Job doesn't end there. He adds:

> But he knows the way that I take;
>   when he has tested me, I shall come out like gold. (Job 23:8-10)

There is a modern echo of all this in Mother Teresa's words: "I know what you feel—terrible longing, with dark emptiness—and yet, he is the one in love with you."

I do not have to go literally forward and backward, right and left, but rather to set out on an inward journey, to seek God *now* and *here*, within and immediately around me. Fundamentally for the monastic person, this journey is the meaning of stability and conversion and obedience. Among the Desert Fathers, whose seeking was a deliberate staying, an "old man" said: "The cell of the monk is the furnace in Babylon, where the three young men found the Son of God: and it is also the pillar of cloud from which God spoke to Moses" (see Daniel 3; Exodus 24).

This life of seeking in faith, in the cloud and in the darkness, on the night shift, is, says Christian mystic Julian of Norwich, "as good as beholding." Though our God is a hidden God (Isaiah 45:15), Paul speaks of "the knowledge of the glory of God in the face of Jesus Christ" (2 Corinthians 4:6)—the Christ who so dominates the mind and heart and Rule of Benedict. And I can seek this face of Christ in his word, his church, his sacraments, the monastic community and all aspects of life within it; in companionship and friendship and love as well as in loneliness; in service and suffering and joy; in everyone I meet and in all creation. But since all these simultaneously conceal and reveal, I must be disposed to see Christ in their depths—and

I become so disposed by desire, expectancy, trust, and an opened heart of gratitude.

How, then, can I open wider and deeper—or reopen—the springs of desire and gratitude and the resultant commitment to seek, which is so fundamental to the gospel and to the Rule by which Benedictine monastics live? How can we, corporately, as community, nurture desire and help sustain in one another the dedication to a genuine seeking? How can we nurture deep and sustained and operative desire in our ministries both within and outside of community? How can we have our desire for God suffuse and transform our administrative responsibilities? How can we share this fundamental dimension of our lives with our guests?

A favorite image of the monastic person in the modern world is as sacrament—an outward and visible sign to others—of desire for God, for God's reign, for the nurturing and extension of God's life and love in the world. It is so easy to have desire eroded, to be diverted or enticed away from that central hunger of our being. We have to keep it *alive*. And how much the church and the world need free men and women of desire, who truly, effectively believe that God seeks *them* in love and desire, and that they will be *found*. Such persons—whether inside or outside the monastery—communicate a constancy of hope, confidence, and joy—not a shallow optimism, but the living fruit of faith. Thus they become, as well, sacraments of thanksgiving and gratitude.

Chapter 2

The Paschal Journey

*T*HE DESIRING AND THE SEEKING set us on a sacred journey. The journey is a common metaphor for the human experience from birth through death. But in the Exodus it becomes a unique and paradigmatic journey—both in the narrow sense of the exodus escape from slavery and in the wider sense of the whole wandering through the wilderness toward a promised land.

Christ assumed and transformed the experience of his people, becoming the New Adam and thus the obedient one—the journeying man who trusted God's promise rather than doubting it—and thus the new Moses, the Son who completed the journey back to his Father by the obedience of love, going through death into fullness of life, and thus becoming the Way for us. Here is a life poured out for all who would receive it, to give life and guidance for their own journey.

And so the Christian is called into the journey and graced for it. Not just in imitation of Christ or even in the common understanding of following Christ, but really, mystically *in* Christ. Our paschal journey, our exodus, is to be accomplished in trusting faith, obedience, willingness to die because we believe in the God of life.

From Death to New Life

We speak so easily, sometimes almost glibly, of "the paschal mystery" of dying and rising. And I discover in pain and dismay that it *is* a mystery. I resist the reality so relentlessly, astonished that God has taken me at my word when I profess to want to follow Christ. I experience the dying and have to trust the rising. But I want to live, and for all my pious words I just don't want to face the truth, the mystery, that to live I must give up "my" life. I must enter into his temptations in my desert and my Gethsemane, in my darkness, weakness, and powerlessness, finally in my death. And I must die not only as he died, but in his death. And really die! Thomas à Kempis suggests that we must be "really dead" to self before we can really live. George MacDonald, whom C. S. Lewis claimed as his master and quoted in almost every book he wrote, said: "You will be dead, so long as you refuse to die."

If Jesus said of himself, "Was it not necessary that the Messiah should suffer these things and then enter into his glory?" (Luke 24:26), and if we want to return to the Father in Jesus to that fullness of life that is glory—do we not have to undergo all this? Or will we say with Peter, "God forbid!"—and get the rebuke Peter got: "Get behind me, Satan!" (Matthew 16:22-23)? It doesn't matter, really, that "these things" to which Jesus refers aren't according to our plans, our projections, our desires. In the process of taking up our cross daily, *as it is given*, we become like him, recover the likeness progressively, become purified, unified, integrated—but oh so slowly and, for many of us, so obscurely.

Simone Weil, an extraordinary and brilliant Jewish woman who died during World War II, said the Cross was enough for her; the Resurrection was her stumbling block. It is no wonder that, though she loved the person of Jesus, loved the Scriptures and the sacraments, and loved much about the church, she would never be baptized. The paschal mystery and the paschal journey are not a matter of dying only—even in the obedience of love. Suffering isn't enough; dying isn't enough. In Paul's words, we would then be "of all people most to be pitied" (1 Corinthians 15:19).

The finality is rising out of that death into newness of life, life beyond our comprehension. For most of us, I suspect, the dying is a matter of experience; the rising, both daily and ultimately, is a matter of faith. And yet it is important to remind ourselves that when it is truly a matter of faith, when we really believe, there is joy. About fifty years ago I came to know Mother Teresa in Calcutta. To have seen her in her first little convent with the few sisters she then had in her community, or to see her with a child who had been rescued from degradation, or with an old man picked up off the streets of Calcutta's indescribable slums so he might die loved, in peace and with dignity—to see her then was to see Christian joy. She lived the paschal mystery in both its facets: dying and transformation in life were written in her face.

Benedict's Paschal Journey

In the *Dialogues* Pope Gregory presents Benedict's paschal journey as a continuous movement toward the Father in Christ and through the gift of their Spirit. Gregory uses a beautiful phrase to express the quality of Benedict's solitude: "He went back to the wilderness he loved, to live alone with himself in the presence of his heavenly Father." And yet, in the paradox—or, far better, the mystery—of Christian life, that very journey into solitude involved him more and more deeply with others.

It has been suggested that the *Dialogues* are plotted primarily upon a geographical rather than a chronological line. From Rome to the gorge of the Anio to the summit of Cassino, Benedict incarnated in his body the journey of his spirit. Along the way, in Alatri, there is a thirteenth-century fresco of the young Benedict with a pilgrim staff in his hand—an Exodus man. And the pilgrimage was literally and spiritually not only a journey but also an ascent. The higher he climbed, the greater his impact on others. This impact was not sought or planned, but simply the rich overflow of a profound and graced human life.

It was a paschal journey for Benedict—a passing over, a dying and rising, a living out of the mystery. We recall his "temptations," but in truth something of Benedict died in each of those purifications, and there was a corresponding transformation. He died to worldly wisdom in Rome, to vanity and ambition in Affile, to sensual desire in that thorn tangle they still point out to visitors and pilgrims at Subiaco, and to aggressiveness and vindictiveness in the affair with Florentius, a neighboring priest who out of envy tried to poison Benedict. Each was a dying; each gave rise to new life, new depth, and these were fruitful in new range and intensity of influence. The climax and summation occurs at the end of Book II of the *Dialogues*. Benedict had long ago "left the world" and yet, thank God and Benedict, he had put much of the earthy into his Rule. Now, at the end, he who had left the world had it given back to him in the transformed unity of a cosmic vision—he saw the world in one single ray of light. "Of course, in saying that the world was gathered up before his eyes I do not mean that heaven and earth grew small, but that his spirit was enlarged. Absorbed as he was in God, it was now easy for him to see all that lay beneath God." Little wonder that Pope John Paul II could say at Monte Cassino some years back, "Come, therefore, O peoples, come to Monte Cassino. Come to learn the true meaning of our earthly pilgrimage; come to regain peace and serenity, tenderness with God and friendship with men."

Gregory speaks truly in saying that Benedict's life and Rule were in harmony—image and paschal mystery together in a life lived and in a way of life bequeathed to others. While the genre of "rule," institutionalizing a way of life, might imply stasis and rigidity, a careful reading of Benedict's Rule demonstrates how very concerned he was with *life*: the phrases "way of life," "light of life," "everlasting life," "way that leads to life" nearly stumble over one another. And when Benedict speaks of community rank, of position, of responsibility, of honor in the community, he does not use prior worldly position, personal gifts, or an array of static "traits" as criteria. Rather, the choice of abbot, of deans, and of overseers of the goods of the monastery, all the determinations about visiting monks and priests in the monastery (and the honorary ranking of monks at the abbot's discretion)—all are based on the dynamic criteria of "manner of life" and "virtuous living."

At any rate, the life Benedict speaks of in the Rule is a paschal life. At the outset of the Prologue he speaks of a return to the Father in an obedience joined to, and empowered by, the paschal obedience of Christ. Within the Prologue he urges: "Clothed then with faith and the performance of good works, let us set out on this way" (21), and "what is not possible to us by nature, ask the Lord to supply by the help of his grace"

The image of God as "Rock" has been dominant
again, and I am taken back to Christ in the Desert
where, for the first time, it took on meaning for me.
The sheer beauty of the rock of those canyon walls,
the sense of "Everlasting Rock." The way in which rock
defines the whole context of life there, the very fact
that the Pueblos and Hispanics thought of it as sacred
ground and were so much in awe (and, apparently, fear)
of those huge rock figures that overlooked the canyon
entrance just outside my door—_los viejos_ on watch.

—_Grace Notes_

(41). The language is intense, urgent, vital: come, run, hasten, progress. He concludes the Prologue with his clearest statement that the monastic life is a paschal life: "Never swerving from his instructions, then, but faithfully observing his teaching in the monastery until death, we shall through patience share in the sufferings of Christ that we may deserve also to share in his kingdom" (50).

The Centrality of Easter

Although there is much that resonates with the paschal mystery intervening between the Prologue and chapter 49, this later chapter seems to pick up the end of the Prologue. "The life of a monk ought to be a continuous Lent" (49:1), Benedict writes; yet, "look forward to holy Easter with joy and spiritual longing" (49:7). The Lent for the Easter; the death for the life. Easter becomes absolutely pivotal and central for every aspect of monastic life. Everything in the monk's life is determined by it: the times for communal prayer, *lectio*, manual work, sleep, vigils, meals, and varied observances. Benedict even has a special chapter (15) on the times for praying Alleluia, the song of Easter joy. Benedict was not asking his followers simply to observe some practices for Lent and some celebration for Easter, but to enter deeply into the paschal mystery—and not only at particular seasons, but as a deepening, lifelong reality intensified, heightened, and renewed periodically in harmony with our being creatures in time.

The Prologue, then, together with chapters 49 and 73, might be called a paschal triptych. It is not so explicit in that final chapter (73), but Benedict does surely imply the paschal journey when he speaks of "the true way to reach the Creator" (73.4) and the need for Christ's help to keep this little Rule for the way (73.8).

Some years ago I spent a year at the Monastery of Christ in the Desert, in New Mexico. It was one of the great joys for me to experience there this centrality of Easter. The monks followed the Rule quite literally in most matters, and such literalism can appear, at first glance, mere antiquarianism. But there is an incommunicable experience of death and life to have Easter so manifestly dominate, to celebrate it in a style of life that is truly Lenten except for that Easter season. To have every activity of your day remind you what time it is in relation to Easter, to have the cycle of seasons and the alternation of darkness and desert light be the setting for the Eucharist and the liturgy of the hours—all this is a paschal setting that vivifies one's liturgical life. Such a seasonal and daily schedule is not possible for most who follow the Rule in this country, but it is good that somewhere it is preserved, not as a museum piece but as a vital testimony to the spiritual riches of the Rule, a blessed quality of earthiness blended inextricably into that spirituality.

Chapter 3

Essentials for the Journey

*I*MMEDIATELY AFTER THE PROLOGUE, which directs us to listen, and thus to know that the way of our seeking is the paschal journey in Christ, Benedict makes clear precisely for whom he is writing: cenobites (from the Greek for "common life") who belong to a monastery in which they live under a rule and an abbot or prioress. Benedict thus provides for two profound human hungers—fundamentally human, not just monastic—and relates them to one another: the hunger for communion with God and with other human beings. The monastic chooses to live *according to* a rule, a Rule that is a specification of the Word of God and of a living tradition, a way of life guided by that Word; *under* an abbot or prioress, a living interpreter of the Word and the tradition; and *in* a community of fellow-seekers, of brothers or sisters in Christ. All three—rule, abbot, community—mediate Christ to the monk and provide the living context in which to seek God.

The Rule is not a compendium of abstract directives, however wise, for reaching even the highest of goals. It is the fruit of a life in intimate communion with God, an invitation to share that life; description of the structures that support the life is secondary. The Rule is written out of Benedict's long experience of living the paschal mystery in the monastic way. The structure is provided for life's sake.

The abbot or prioress is the living spiritual father or mother, the abba or amma, teacher, shepherd, and physician. The Rule's principal directive for the abbot or prioress seems to be to care—not simply to preserve life according to the gospel and the Rule, or to preserve the distinct charism of the community, but to nurture the members of the community, to bring them to greater realization, corporately and in each individual. It is important to note that this can be done only in the measure of the community's faith—the Rule says the abbot or prioress is *believed* to hold the place of Christ in the community.

The community itself, as Cardinal Basil Hume has said, is "an affirmation of God." It is a communion in faith and therefore a communion in the Spirit. It is founded on an ecclesial model, not a purely sociological one, and the brothers or sisters are therefore truly members of one another. The late Brother Roger Schutz of Taizé wrote this: "We simply wanted to bring together men who would commit themselves to following Christ in order to be a living sign of the unity of the church. Life in community is an image of the total reality of the church; and the sign of a life in common, however humble it may be in itself, has a power which far surpasses the limitations of the men who make it up." It is a graced community of faith, of mutual service, and mutual confirmation in seeking God—a "school for the Lord's service" (Prologue 45).

Chapters 4–7 of the Rule indicate the essentials that are to be learned in this school, first in a general listing of the tools of good works, and then in three discrete chapters on obedience, restraint of speech, and humility. These are virtues of Christ himself, and are far more surely and authentically acquired by those who seek to be possessed by Christ than by those who seek to possess the virtues.

The interrelation and interdependence of obedience, restraint of speech, and humility are made clear by Benedict's assigning three steps of humility to obedience and three steps to silence. Though not separable, these three monastic virtues can be distinguished.

OBEDIENCE, DISCERNING GOD'S WILL

Benedict had already spoken of the paschal obedience of Christ and the monk in the Prologue, as he knew it from living with the Scriptures. We know from those Scriptures the disobedience of God's people and the consequences. We know God's unfailing fidelity throughout the history of our infidelities. We know, finally, the perfect obedience of a Son, one for whom obedience was not conformity with the prescriptions of law but a passion to discover and carry out the beloved will of his Father as that will was to direct his life. His was truly the "new heart" of Jeremiah's and Ezekiel's promise. Jesus was constantly turned toward his Father, open to his Father, and could thus discern the Father's will. He demonstrated this, for instance, in healing on the Sabbath, even when that healing seemed to the professional religious leaders of his time a violation of God's law (John 5). In seeking God's will rather than being merely bound by the externals of law, Jesus was the truly obedient one. And, it is important to note, Jesus was obedient to his Father's will not only when he perceived it internally but also when that will was truly mediated through his human relationships—his parents, legitimate authority, the concrete demands of daily life, even the coin of Caesar.

The Letter to the Hebrews (10:9) tells us that Christ said: "See, I have come to do your will." As a consequence of Jesus' living this out, the same letter (5:8-9) says of him: "Although he was a Son, he learned obedience through what he suffered; and having been made perfect, he became the source of eternal salvation for all who obey him."

Monastic obedience is a flowering of this evangelical obedience. It arose in the church out of a desire to obey the will of God and out of a conviction that, for some at least, God's will is known most surely through submission in faith to another human being and to a community of fellow seekers who may see through my blind spots and past my self-imposed limitations, who may open my motives to purification, who may help me distinguish my ego from my true self. And, in helping to discern God's will for me, they will support me through my weakness to the fulfilling of that will of God.

Among the Desert Fathers and Mothers there is an abundance of "words of life" about obedience. Amma Syncletica said: "As long as we are in the monastery, obedience is preferable to asceticism. The one teaches pride, the other humility." One of the lesser known, Abba Hyperechius, said: "Obedience is the best ornament of the monk. Whoever has acquired it will be heard by God, and will stand beside the crucified with confidence, for the crucified Lord became obedient unto death." And the great Abba Pambo

I told the novice mistress, Sister Alcuin (who was hard on me, good to me, good for me), that there were two things I just couldn't do in the years ahead: I couldn't stand to go teach in the orphanage in St. Paul (I had visited it as part of a sociology class trip and had been repelled by the regimentation of the children), and I couldn't live with Sister X, much older, forbidding, obviously without any patience for or trust in this young nun. Near the end of the year in the novitiate I was assigned to the orphanage, and Sister X was transferred there.

—*Grace Notes*

of Scete reflected upon tales of the virtue of four monks. One was a serious faster, another practiced rigorous poverty, the third acquired profound charity, and the fourth lived for twenty-two years in obedience to his spiritual father. Pambo said: "I tell you, the virtue of this last one is the greatest. Each of the others has obtained the virtue he wished to acquire; but the last one, restraining his own will, does the will of another. Now it is of such men that the martyrs are made, if they persevere to the end."

Obedience as a Response to Seeking God

It is, Benedict says, "by this way of obedience that we go to God" (71:2). The monk must clearly try to see obedience as both baptismal and monastic. It is radically and essentially an obedience to God, an obedience of faith. But we are embodied spirits, and obedience to God is mediated by obedience shown to those who, in respect to us, share in God's authority. For, says Benedict, "the obedience shown to superiors is given to God" (5:15). As well as being an obedience of faith, it is an obedience of hope and love too. And for those who love Christ above all, Benedict says, unhesitating obedience comes naturally (5:2).

All in the monastery must be obedient to God, to the gospel, and to the Rule. From this flows a beautiful mutual influx throughout the community. The monastic is to obey the abbot or prioress, and the real quality of this obedience is best expressed in Benedict's saying that at the same moment the directive is given the monastic responds, and "both actions together are swiftly completed as one" (5:9). This does not suggest the dominance of a master and the servility of a subject, but collaboration. It is an echo of the conversation between God and the believer in the Prologue (15-16): "*Is there anyone here who yearns for life and desires to see good days?* (Ps 33[34]:13)" and the response, "I do!"

For their part, the abbot and prioress are to be obedient to the unique and vital charism of their particular communities, to the baptismal and monastic vocation of each member of the monastery, and they must truly listen to the voice of the Spirit in the community and its deliberations.

The community members must be obedient to each other (71). This too, is an obedience of trusting faith and of love. By commitment in community, monks insert themselves by the grace of God into a specific living tradition, an ongoing and developing tradition, and must listen to it with their hearts at its heart, be true to it and responsible for it.

Within this mutuality, in this heartbeat of the community, it is the vocation and life and growth and holiness of each person that is of primary concern. Because it is this monk's obedience to God, the monk and the abbot and the community must be sensitive to and responsive to this individual person's unique call within the community. Correspondingly, the monk must listen with the ear of the heart to the abbot and the other monks for help in discerning the will of God amid all the conflicting signals from ego and surroundings. This is essential to seeking God, and is both one of the requirements for acceptance into the community—the applicant should be eager for obedience—and the content of one of the solemn promises in this community.

Love Motivates Obedience

Of all the motives that Benedict lists for obedience (5:3, 9, 13)—dread of hell, the fact that monks have professed (and are thus bound by) a holy service, fear of the Lord, the imitation of Christ, desire for everlasting life—it is to love he returns again and again: the love that motivated Jesus' obedience, and the love into which we should be growing day by day in monastic life.

Benedict not only places obedience before us as a requirement and an ideal, urging us to the highest motivation, but also specifies the qualities of that obedience—cheerful, whole-hearted, total, trusting, prompt, patient, and persevering.

There are, of course, times in our personal lives and in the course of history when obedience seems especially difficult. Brother Roger of Taizé indicated that he had not used the word "obedience" in his entire Rule because in the mid-1960s it roused so much negative response. He does, however, have a chapter on acceptance of authority, and he writes: "Without unity, there is no hope for bold and total service of Jesus Christ. Individualism breaks up the community and brings it to a halt." And he says it is the role of authority to focus the community's unity.

When the call to obedience seems burdensome and insupportable in an age of assertiveness and self-fulfillment, the observations of so great an individualist as the nineteenth-century Lutheran, Søren Kierkegaard, may be of more help than pious exhortations. In his journals he wrote: "Every human being would be infinitely powerful if he did not need to use two-thirds of his energy in finding his task." And again: "Every human being who has even once understood himself penetratingly understands further that he could never possibly be satisfied with being the master of his fate, that for a human being there is satisfaction and joy and blessedness only in obeying."

For my own perception of this matter of obedience, I have in recent years joined Augustine's famous phrase, "Unless you believe, you shall not understand," to Dietrich Bonhoeffer's assertion, reflecting on Christ's command to Peter to come to him on the water (Matthew 14:28-29), "Unless he obeys, a man cannot believe." This provides increasingly effective insight for me, especially when obedience is difficult.

Benedict himself assures us that if we are faithful, obedience will become increasingly less burdensome; and though the entry is by the narrow road that makes for hard going, the way opens out, even in this life, and we come to find life and joy on the way. "But as we progress in this way of life and in faith, we shall run on the path of God's commandments, our hearts overflowing with the inexpressible delight of love" (Prologue 49).

Obedience Leads to Freedom of Spirit

It is a paradox or, much better, mystery, that freedom is inherent in true obedience. As fullness of life is the other side of death in the paschal mystery, so liberty of spirit is the other side of responsible and genuine obedience.

Jesus came to liberate and did so by obedience. He was a majestically free man precisely in being profoundly obedient. Incorporated into his sonship, we participate both in his obedience and in the freedom of the children of God.

This freedom of spirit, of the Spirit, is treasured by obedient monks. One of the Desert Fathers spoke to his disciple about the varied ways followed by men of the Old Testament—Abraham, Elijah, and David—whose relationship with God had schooled their hearts. He then said to his disciple: "Do whatever you see your soul desires according to God and guard your heart." This is reminiscent of Augustine's "Love and do what you will." Either statement can surely be distorted, but—just as surely—when one's heart has been long-schooled in a genuine seeking to love God, then one has the radical freedom to do one's own will, now freely united with and conformed to the liberating will of God.

Benedict demonstrates this freedom in his Rule. There was a wide range of rules and teachings open to him in the monastic tradition, and though he loved that tradition, he was not a slave to any of it. The Rule shows wide influence but is, in the end, a very personal document.

Benedict is free in the use of Scripture; it was so internalized that his use is a spillover, in harmony with the whole even when it is not precise quotation. He is free in being firm in spiritual matters such as obedience and humility, the eradication of private ownership, the regularity of the daily office and *lectio*; and he is flexible in such material considerations as personal needs, food, the details of the work of God. Similarly he is free in leaving much to the discretion of the abbot or prioress, who is not a mere functionary but a Spirit person. Immediately after saying that the abbot is believed to hold the place of Christ, he refers to Romans 8:15: "*You have received the spirit of adoption of sons*" (2:2-3). This may apply not only to the abbot but to the freedom, both Christian and monastic, of the monks who believe the abbot does hold the place of Christ.

In contrast to the practice of his time—and of most times since, including our own, in both ecclesial and public life—Benedict demonstrates a freedom of spirit in providing for the counsel of the entire community. This is not just to survey competencies in the community, but to allow the Spirit to speak charismatically, by the gifts of the Spirit in community members, when the institutional element might inhibit action. All through the Rule, and most evidently in speaking of the private prayer of the monk, Benedict is careful not to stifle the spiritual liberty of each one by legislation that is too precise. And he leaves so much open to future interpretation and adaptation.

This is a genuine and life-giving freedom, not a life-denying self-centeredness and self-assertion. It is truly the liberty of the sons and daughters of God. George MacDonald wrote, "It is because we are not near enough to thee to partake of thy liberty that we want a liberty of our own different from thine." And Jean Leclercq said of Benedict, "His is the gift to be totally dependent and entirely free. He obeys God and the Church with a sovereign mastery."

Thomas Merton speaks of the monastic freedom of Benedict's followers:

> The world needs men who are free from its demands, men who are not alienated by its servitudes in any way. The monastic vocation is traditionally regarded as a charism of liberty in which the monk does not simply turn his back upon the world, but on the contrary becomes free with the perfect freedom of the sons of God by virtue of the fact that, having followed Christ into the wilderness and shared in his temptations and sufferings, he can also follow him wherever else he may go.

SILENCE, OR REVERENCE FOR SPEECH

We will have much to say of silence in Part II of this book. In the meantime, we need to understand how silence works in Benedict's overall design of a life for seeking God.

If I am to heed Scripture's "Hear O Israel!" and Benedict's "Listen!"— if I am to be obedient in this root sense—I must be silent enough to truly hear. Out of our wordiness there now seems to have developed a thirst for solitude and silence again. We have begun to realize that dialogue of itself is not the total solution. It is in fruitful, reflective, and prayerful silence that we come to some real measure of depth, clarity, rootedness, and cohesion. Otherwise, we are batting the air.

Scripture speaks of silence before God's word, before God's mystery. Often silence—exterior and interior quiet—is clearly indicated or implied as requisite to hearing God's word, being aware of God's presence, being sufficiently present to ourselves to recognize God's presence within and among us. "Be still and know that I am God" (Psalm 46:10).

But silence is not an end in itself. It is for the word—to hear the word with the ear of the heart, to let it enter deeply and fully, and then to speak out of that depth in loving response. There is "a time to keep silence, and a time to speak" (Ecclesiastes 3:7).

The Desert Fathers and Mothers were always being asked for a word of life. Although their answers, like Jesus' own, come down to us chiseled by tradition, the representation is probably not far from the truth. Jesus and the abbas and ammas who were deeply formed in his word were men and women of few words, but words spoken with power. Benedict reflects the same tradition and spirit. He said nothing to us of himself except what we can discern from his Rule. Jean Leclercq says it is because Benedict is such a model of silence, especially about himself, that we find it necessary to speak so much about him.

In older English translations, Benedictine "taciturnity" was called "silence," and in *RB 1980* it is entitled "restraint of speech." If one were not translating a title but making one up out of the whole cloth of the Rule, it might well be "Reverence for Speech." Benedict does legislate silence, but the texts in which he speaks of the wise and loving use of words considerably outweigh those in which he mandates silence.

"There are times when good words are to be left unsaid out of esteem for silence" (6:2), and "monks should diligently cultivate silence at all times, but especially at night" (42:1). These very admonitions, in the light of the whole Rule, seem directed at the reverent use of speech rather than simple repression of it, or reluctance to speak when speech is called for. Think of the abbot's or prioress's use of speech in dealing with the varied personalities in the monastery, of his role as teacher by word as well as example, of her dealing with the erring sister, and in so many relations with the community and guests. And what Benedict says of the abbot or prioress is, proportionately, his ideal for every monastic. Think, too, of the guest master, the porter, the cellarer, the *senpectae* (the spiritual elders in the monastery)—Benedict gives directives about speech for each of them. The community members are to express their opinions appropriately when the community is called to counsel, and they are reminded that they may speak up when asked to do what is difficult and burdensome or seemingly impossible.

Many of the restrictions on speech are for the sake of charity—on leaving the oratory after the Work of God so that others may pray undisturbed, at night, at table, outside the oratory during Office, during the time of *lectio* or siesta. Even readers and chanters are to be chosen with an eye or an ear to charity. Not to be able to speak with community members is considered appropriate punishment for faults, as is prohibition of using one's power of speech to pray aloud in the community. Benedict is almost at his most severe with that misuse of speech: grumbling. All this indicates real reverence for speech, not merely a negative concern about silence.

Ambrose Wathen, OSB, says that the word "taciturn" might well come from the Sanskrit root meaning "to satisfy," to be at rest, inwardly quiet. Our situation today is hardly to be at rest. We are full of racket within, the din of our egos. All too often we take refuge in noise or words, sometimes almost unconsciously, to escape from inner abysses and outer tensions that we lack the courage, or perhaps even the fundamental honesty, to face. For the most part the words we utter in such situations are empty.

If to be at rest, instead of uncommunicative and withdrawn, is indeed the meaning of silence, we need to rethink Benedict's use of the term. His silence, then, would have very positive resonance.

HUMILITY, AN EXERCISE IN AUTHENTICITY

Humility has not had very good press lately, yet Christian and monastic identity are eroded by every diminution of true humility.

We hardly need to recall what we know so well from Scripture, and yet we cannot ruminate it often enough. We know that it is the humble of Israel who were open to God, knowing how deeply they needed God; that the Israelites had constantly to be humbled so that they could and would truly seek God again; that, as the Book of Judith (9:11) has it, God is "the God of the lowly"; that, as Hannah prayed, "He raises up the poor from the dust; he lifts the needy from the ash heap" (1 Samuel 2:8); that it is the humble, like the mysterious Servant of the Lord (Isaiah 52–53), who can and do truly love.

In Jesus we see the perfection of this self-emptying openness to God, this infinite capacity to serve in love. And I who am his disciple am called to humility by all those Scriptures I know so well, use so often, and all too frequently would like to demythologize to soften the blow, to sterilize out any real personal significance and binding power. "Let the same mind be in you that was in Christ Jesus, who . . . emptied himself" (Philippians 2:5-7). "All of you must clothe yourselves with humility in your dealings with one another. . . . Humble yourselves therefore under the mighty hand of God, so that he may exalt you in due time" (1 Peter 5:5-6). "Do not be haughty, but associate with the lowly; do not claim to be wiser than you are" (Romans 12:16).

I have become increasingly attracted to the very statement that used to scandalize me most: "Whoever becomes humble like this child . . . " (Matthew 18:4). Sigrid Undset, Scandinavian convert and novelist, wrote that one vision persists throughout the literature and dreams of the Middle Ages—that when the Antichrist comes he will suddenly appear as a full-grown man. The Antichrist would not dare to make himself so small as to be born of a woman, play on the streets of an obscure village, be dependent on simple and lowly people.

There is a profound perception here that has bearing on our lives: humility is a godly virtue. To become as little children—small, poor, transparent, dependent, receiving all as gift, capable of surprise and wonder and growth—Kierkegaard, reflecting on the gospel demand, wrote: "To *be* a child . . . when one simply is such is an easy thing; but the *second time*—the second time is decisive. To become again a child . . . —that is the task."

The early monastic tradition is rich in teaching about and exhorting to humility. In the terse language of the Desert Fathers we read that a certain elder said, "If you see a young monk by his own will climbing up into heaven, take him by the foot and throw him to the ground, because what he is doing is not good for him." They tell of one desert man who fasted for seventy weeks and pored over the Scriptures all that time, seeking the meaning of a text and getting nowhere on his own, or even with the aid of his prayers and fasting. "Look at all the work I have done without getting anywhere! I will go to one of the brothers and ask him." He had no more than closed the door on his way out when the Scripture was opened to him.

Pachomius instructed his followers: "Above all this, we have been given humility, which watches over all the virtues and is that great holy strength with which God clothed himself when he came into the world. Humility is the rampart of the virtues, the treasury of works, the saving armor and the cure for every wound. . . . Humility is least among men, but precious and glorious before God." And Dorotheus of Gaza said humility is the lime, taken out of the earth (*humus*), to bind together each and every stone of our spiritual edifice. Without this lime, this cement, the whole will collapse.

The principal concern of monastics, after Scripture, is the Rule under which they live. Benedict's seventh chapter is echoed throughout the

Rule; humility is mentioned in twenty of the seventy-two chapters. The frequency, however, is not important—the pervasive quality is. Benedict begins chapter 7 with a note of urgency: "Divine Scripture calls to us saying: *'Whoever exalts himself shall be humbled, and whoever humbles himself shall be exalted'*" (7:1; citing Luke 14:11). Monastics are to be humble in their relations with God, within the community, and with guests. Humility is to characterize each monastic, and specific explicit demands are made on the abbot or prioress, the cellarer, the readers, the novices, the porter, those who make mistakes in the oratory, the excommunicated, the artisans, the priests of the community or those who want to join it, and visiting monks.

All of this is not exterior piety but recognition of the truth of one's condition, an exercise in authenticity. For example, in the seventh step the monk "not only admits with his tongue but is also convinced in his heart" (7:51), and in the twelfth step the monk "manifests humility in his bearing no less than in his heart" (7:62).

The Degrees of Humility

The twelve degrees of humility move from interior disposition to external expression. The first is to fear the Lord, to keep in one's heart the reverential awe of God that underlies all the rest. The last is, as we noted, always to manifest humility in one's bearing no less than in one's heart. The insistence of Benedict's phrases is striking: never forget, constantly remember, keep in mind (7:10-11).

The degrees of humility may be analyzed in many ways, but Benedict is writing a Rule for monastic persons to live by, not to diagram. It may be said that the first five steps in humility, which are interior, dispose the monastic to total readiness to do God's will, with the fifth step, in which the monastic confesses to his spiritual father or her spiritual mother, bridging from interior to exterior. The sixth and seventh steps are the other side of that readiness for God: distrust of self, rejection of self-love and self-seeking. And the last five steps manifest the spirit of simplicity and interiority that characterize the monastic deeply formed and matured in monastic life. It is again that mystery of life in Christ, echoing death and life, obedience and freedom. Here we climb downward to ascend, echoing the complete reversal of values Jesus holds before his followers in the Beatitudes. It is a syllabus for a lifetime in the school of the Lord's service. In the process the heart is purified, the capacity for perfect love expanded, and the possession of true freedom increasingly realized. Benedict makes this explicit in that beautiful conclusion that never becomes worn out by use:

> Now, therefore, after ascending all these steps of humility, the monk will quickly arrive at that *perfect love* of God which *casts out fear* (1 John 4:18). Through this love, all that he once performed with dread, he will now begin to observe without effort, as though naturally, from habit, no longer out of fear of hell, but out of love for Christ, good habit and delight in virtue. All this the Lord will by the Holy Spirit graciously manifest in his workman now cleansed of vices and sins. (7:67-70)

This conclusion to chapter 7 in itself echoes the end of the Prologue, and the two together enclose the heart of the Rule. This fundamental fact about a Benedictine way to God was eloquently stated by Cardinal Basil Hume, OSB, when he spoke to the general chapter of the American Cassinese Congregation in 1980:

> The monk knows deep-down that he is not what he should be, not just in terms of his monastic vocation, but as a human being like everyone else. It takes some years of experience in monastic life to recognize that consciousness of failure and frailty must not lead to despondency, but rather to complete trust and confidence in God's help. We have to move from preoccupation with our own perfection to an intense interest in the perfection of God. . . .
>
> The abyss of our nothingness has to be filled with the immensity of God's love. Humility is a lovable virtue—delightful to observe in others; painfully difficult to acquire for oneself. But it is the only way to get the relationships in the monastery right: that is, between God and ourselves on the one hand, and between the brethren on the other. Proud men cannot live together in peace. . . .
>
> How very important it is to recognize that humility, as St. Benedict understands it, is a whole attitude of mind. The false idea that the humble man is, in some way, an emaciated person, limp and negative, would have been far from his thought. On the contrary, humility is a virtue for the strong monk, because it enables him to put God and other people at the center of his life, and not

himself. It should release the powers and energies with which God has endowed him, and make him a valuable instrument in the service of the Lord.

The humble monk is the monk with authentic dignity—a person like his Master, who could say, "learn from me; for I am gentle and humble in heart" (Matthew 11:29), and who could thus stand in strength and dignity and full self-possession before Pilate, before his persecutors, before all the proud and ambitious men of his time, and yet was at home with the lowly or the outcast and treated the sinner with healing love.

PRAYER, DRAWING THE MIND INTO THE HEART

We have dealt with virtues Benedict considers fundamental to monastic life—obedience and silence and humility—all three grounded in the paschal mystery and with love as the motivation for each. Benedict then presents activities that presuppose and need these virtues: prayer and *lectio*. Obedience, silence, humility, prayer, and *lectio* are deeply and delicately related to each other, and when they are really practiced and in balance, monastic life flourishes. Conversely, when one or more is neglected, overstressed, or gets out of phase with the rest, monastic life— and hence ecclesial life, the life of the church—suffers.

In speaking of prayer of the monastic person, we will consider only so-called "private prayer," though the term can be misleading. No prayer of the Christian is really private, but if we use "personal," the implication is that somehow the monk's liturgical prayer is not personal. There seems to be no alternative but to speak of "private" prayer.

First, prayer is simply *there*, provided for in the structure of monastic life from the beginning. Monastics are raised on it, and it is a constant experiential presence for them to respond to.

Second, the monastic is to be a person of prayer, and this presupposes that the specified times of prayer in common overflow into and are nourished by "private prayer." The fourth-century Syrian *Book of Degrees* specifies three stages of the liturgy—the liturgy of the community, the liturgy of the heart, and the liturgy of heaven. Midway between the communal liturgy and the heavenly liturgy is the interiorized liturgy of the praying heart.

Third is the hunger of God's people today, people of every age, for an authentic and deep private prayer. And they need help. Monastics who truly seek to pray can give that help in an almost unique way. In the flood of "how to" books and techniques, the search sometimes seems to be for experience instead of for God, threatening to separate prayer from life. The school of the Lord's service helps monastics help others.

It is noteworthy that the gospels, especially Luke, describe Jesus praying in the hills and in the desert. Though his presence in the temple and at feasts is often noted, and surely his presence there was prayer, it is not there that the evangelists expressly speak of his praying. "He would withdraw to deserted places and pray" (Luke 5.16).

The monastic ideal of unceasing prayer is based on Luke 18 and 1 Thessalonians 5—indeed, it is a general Christian ideal, since these passages were written for all followers of Christ. It may seem surprising on the face of it that the desert monks do not say much about prayer. Abba Agathon did say that of all the good works, "I think there is no labor greater than that of prayer to God." And Epiphanius of Cyprus, told by a visiting abbot, rather smugly, that his monks religiously keep the "appointed round of psalmody," responded, "It is clear that you do not trouble about the other hours of the day, if you cease from prayer. The true monk should have prayer and psalmody continually in his heart."

Benedict would have agreed with Agathon and Epiphanius. Although Gregory's *Dialogues* surely give glimpses of a man who prayed, a contemplative by any measure, Benedict says very little in the Rule about private prayer and he offers no method for it. The Rule, written in the midst of a tradition, assumes what went before it and was communicated through living example, and Benedict has great reverence for the work of the Spirit in prayer and for the freedom of the monastic person to pray as the Spirit leads.

The most obvious reason the Rule says little about private prayer, however, is that Benedict is concerned with a whole life of prayer, with becoming prayer. The entire Rule provides for a way of life, a schooled receptivity to grace, a disciplined availability to God that will open out a life of prayer and make the monastic a living prayer. Saint Benedict flies in the face of some "how to" books—here is no state of the art technique but a demanding, long-term schooling that reaches into every aspect of a person's life to open it, often painfully, and transform it into prayer.

Learning to Draw the Mind into the Heart

That becoming prayer is a life work is evident from the fact that chapters 20 (Reverence in Prayer) and 52 (The Oratory of the Monastery) are so brief in themselves; obviously a great deal is presumed. It is also evident from the fact that invitations to prayer, even apart from the references to the Divine Office, which take up about one-seventh of the Rule, appear throughout Benedict's directives for monastic life.

Verse 4 of the Prologue declares that every good work is to begin in prayer. As the Prologue continues, there is dialogue between God and the seeking monk, a model of prayer (14-19). The tools of good works direct the monk to devote himself often to prayer (4:57). The monk is to "remember God," and to greet Christ in everyone he meets. He is to pray with guests. Benedict surely implies unceasing prayer in chapter 7, where the monk is directed to "[keep] the *fear of God* always *before his eyes* (Ps 35[36]:2)" (7:10) and to "constantly say in his heart what the publican in the Gospel said with downcast eyes: *Lord, I am a sinner, not worthy to look up to heaven* (Luke 18:13)" (7:65).

Those two short chapters, 20 and 52, and the relevant verses of chapter 49 on Lent, are especially rich in implication for the private prayer of the monk. In the five short verses of chapter 20, Benedict specifies several times that prayer should be pure. Although some monastic savants argue about the precise meaning, it would seem we can settle for something like heartfelt, genuine, undivided. Benedict says prayer must be humble and out of sincere devotion. In harmony with monastic tradition, he says it should be short, "unless perhaps it is prolonged under the inspiration of divine grace" (20:4). And prayer should be with purity of heart and compunction—repentance sharpened by desire.

Chapter 52:4 provides us with that chaste and lovely phrase, "he may simply go in and pray," quietly, "with tears and heartfelt devotion." And in chapter 49 the reference is short but rich. The monk is encouraged to add to his usual service during Lent by private prayer and abstinence. Benedict invites us to offer this prayer in the joy of the Holy Spirit.

While there is no explicit reference to prayer in the concluding chapter, it is an extraordinary invitation to prayer. It is as if Benedict stood at the door of his school on commencement day and opened it wide on the promise of life, fullness of life—the fullness of being prayer.

Thus, prayer in the Rule is like prayer in Luke's Gospel; it is there at beginning and end and the whole is suffused with it. And this life of prayer in the Rule is nourished by the liturgy, by *lectio*, table reading, and by work. It is indeed a school of the Lord's service.

And the school is not mainly for our heads. It is principally our hearts that need to be educated, activated, and released. The monks of the East use a rich phrase: to stand before God with the mind in the heart. Theophan the Recluse says that when thoughts of God are in the head they are "outside" and prayer remains "exterior." To learn to draw the mind into the heart, to the very core of one's being and interiority, thus unifying one's powers at their center, is to recognize God within—the baptismal gift. Theophan recommends that we never conclude prayer without arousing some real response to God. As George MacDonald has said, "Nothing is so deadening to the divine as an habitual dealing with the outside of holy things." Again, Theophan says that he who has zeal to pray needs no teaching on how to become perfect in prayer. "Patiently continued, the effort of prayer itself will lead us to prayer's very summit." And words of noted nineteenth-century London Baptist preacher Charles H. Spurgeon express how the disposition of remembering God affects the way we do our work and enjoy our leisure: "Prayer should be the key of the day and the lock of the night."

LECTIO, READING SO THAT THE WHOLE PERSON IS ENGAGED

Benedict doesn't say a great deal about *lectio*. The Rule is itself a product of *lectio*. The more one reads and ponders and studies the Rule, the more evident this becomes. But Benedict does provide a great deal of time for *lectio* (several hours a day, more in Lent, and the best hours of the day at every season). He speaks of it very briefly in chapter 4 on the tools of good works: "Listen readily to holy reading" (4:55), and then treats it at greater length in chapter 48 on manual labor. But he deals with it there only in the sense that he regulates the times for *lectio* at various seasons in conjunction with determining work time. In reality, *lectio* is much more closely related to prayer than to work, laborious as it may sometimes be.

The fact that Benedict says relatively little about an exercise for which he provides a great deal of time is simply because it was part of the lived monastic tradition and needed no explanation. The earlier Pachomian Rules do have more explicit things to say: "There shall be no one whatever in the monastery who does not learn to read and does not memorize something of the Scriptures." The monks were expected to memorize at least the New Testament and the Psalter. "At work, they shall talk of no worldly matter, but either recite holy things or else keep silent." And the monks are exhorted by Horsiesios: "Let us be wealthy in texts learned by heart."

It is evident that for Benedict the subject matter of *lectio* is Scripture. Works that throw light on the Scriptures or the monastic life are also *lectio* materials, as is evident in chapter 73, where he refers to "the holy catholic Fathers," the *Conferences*, the *Institutes*, and the *Lives* of the Fathers, and the Rule of Basil. The method, if one may call it that, is to read in such a way that the whole person is engaged. Much was committed to memory and then, as is evident from the Pachomian texts, these were repeated at manual work and when time allowed until they had really become deeply engraved in consciousness.

This simple process and the explanation of it were developed through the centuries. The most detailed description according to discrete stages was probably the work of the Carthusian abbot, Guigo II, in the late twelfth-century classic, *The Ladder of Monks*.

Lectio, Meditatio, Oratio, Contemplatio

Jean Leclercq's work has made the four steps widely known in our time. The four (*lectio, meditatio, oratio, contemplatio*) are normally, but not necessarily, a sequence—the Holy Spirit is not programmed by our stages and categories. In so far as it is a sequence, Saint John of the Cross has stated it most succinctly: "Seek in reading and you will find in meditation; knock in prayer and it will be opened to you in contemplation."

The *lectio* itself is a type of reading, primarily of the Word of God, that is a listening with the ears of the heart, a seeking and savoring, a kind of incarnation of the Word of God in this time and place that calls for deep reverence and receptivity. It is a slow reading with no concern to get a certain amount accomplished. If possible, the text should be read aloud. Guigo speaks of it as putting whole food into the mouth, inviting tasting, masticating. William of St. Thierry, an earlier contemporary of Guigo, suggests in the *Golden Epistle* that such reading should not be haphazard, but planned, concentrating on certain authors until one has a profound familiarity with them.

Meditatio follows, and seems to be of two basic types. The simpler is a committing to memory, then heart, and then a simple repetition, a murmuring in a deep receptivity to the text, such as a psalm verse. It is likened to the ruminating process in animals, and early Christian writers pointed out that the ruminants were the clean animals of Leviticus and Deuteronomy. William of St. Thierry says the text for rumination should be something that will really hold the attention and lead to progressively deeper familiarity.

The second type of *meditatio* seems closer to study, what Guigo calls an application of the mind in search of the truth of the text. There is evidence, in this more intellectual approach, of the situation in Guigo's time—the rise of universities, the beginnings of scholastic theology. But Guigo speaks of a pondering that gives rise to longing, and thus distinguishes it from an exclusively or even primarily intellectual approach.

An illuminating example of *meditatio* in yet another mode is provided by Rudolf Koch, the German artist. Reading Scripture, apparently after his conversion, he was overwhelmed and began to copy it. But this did not seem durable enough. "The words required to be experienced in all their weight. Then I began to engrave them in metal, to sculpture them in wood, to embroider them and weave them in tapestry; they were painted in frescoes and poured in bronze. And it is not the end; because these words always penetrate deeper into the one who has been captured by them. What is more, he is entirely transformed by them; life finds its meaning and death loses its fear."

Oratio arises from the murmuring, or the searching, or whatever the mode of *meditatio*. Benedict virtually says this in the sequence of two statements in the tools for good works: "Listen readily to holy reading, and devote yourself often to prayer" (4:55-56). William of St. Thierry says the reading should stimulate the feelings, and reading is thus interrupted by prayer—an interruption, he says, "which should not so much hamper the reading as restore to it a mind ever more purified for understanding." Guigo observes that the more the monk meditates, the deeper his longing and his awareness of need for God's help, and thus he asks for the good he sees through *lectio* and *meditatio* but cannot obtain of himself. Obviously, the asking does not have to be in words. The simple longing, desire, is itself prayer, as Guigo says so beautifully.

Surely, however, the prayer to which *meditatio* gives rise is not only petition. Thanksgiving, praise, compunction can arise as well out of a heart that has been deeply moved. Whatever the type of prayer, Benedict would say it should be short, sincere, pure, humble.

The steps of *lectio, meditatio,* and *oratio,* are available to every Christian. *Contemplatio,* as used here, is wholly God's gift. The Holy Spirit has been increasingly active in the previous three steps; now the activity is clearly that of the Spirit. *Contemplatio* can be described as a unifying, deeply loving awareness analogous to a profound experience of beauty. Guigo says that by one's own prayer in *oratio,* desire for God becomes inflamed. And in this fourth stage God breaks in on that desire and satisfies it. Essentially *contemplatio* is an awareness or an experience, usually very brief, of the intimate, active, and transforming presence of God. God may or may not give the awareness. Our hunger is for God rather than for an experience of God.

Lectio, Study, and Spiritual Reading

Lectio differs from both study and spiritual reading. Unlike study, *lectio* is not for intellectual knowledge, mastery, usefulness. It is not primarily an exercise of the critical faculties, though to have exercised them previously on the text to the best of one's abilities is surely desirable. It leads to a different kind of immersion and assimilation, a making oneself available to be shaped and reshaped in one's deepest being. Guigo writes: "You will have understood to no purpose unless you love what you understand, for wisdom consists in love. For understanding goes before the spirit of wisdom, and receives only a passing taste; but love savors solid food. It is

VESPER SPARROW

*P*oised:
on a brown reed
against the flaming sun
she sings,
with grace and urgency of praise,
a small brown bird's
Magnificat.

—*Grace Notes*

in love that all the strength of the soul consists, it is into love that all life-giving nourishment flows, it is from love that life is poured into every limb and gives it power." And yet, though *lectio* differs from study, it deeply affects study. The witness to this is what Jean Leclercq has called "monastic theology" and the whole culture of the monastic centuries. There is evidence of hunger for its revival today, an invitation to us to give what is, or can be, a uniquely monastic gift to others.

Lectio differs also from spiritual reading. The latter is generally from a wider range, and usually calls for a single reading done straight-on rather than made a subject of *meditatio*. Spiritual reading is often pursued for practical application, perhaps one's own program of self-improvement. Surely portions of what one chooses for spiritual reading may often serve for *lectio*.

Lectio, an activity energized by the Holy Spirit, cannot be programmed, but there are things we can do to increase our receptivity to the Spirit's initiative:

• Try to ready yourself by being quiet and receptive. Do not always choose for *lectio* those texts or books that attract you and please you in your present state. *Lectio* is meant to open us up and transform us.

• Wholly and deliberately encourage the confrontation with your life that *lectio* produces, and be ready for the change or growth it demands.

• Do *lectio* regularly, preferably at a set time and at a quiet, leisurely pace, letting the *meditatio* and *oratio* "interrupt" as they will.

• The choice of place is important—a place that is used regularly so that it disposes you immediately for what you are about to do. It should of itself provide a suitable atmosphere and not be distracting. Or, you can introduce some element that serves to transform a regular environment, such as a candle lighted before an icon in your room specifically and only for *lectio*.

• Follow the example of the early monks, using the body as much as possible: alert, relaxed posture; reading aloud if possible and listening as well as seeing; using prayerful gesture in the *oratio* if you are attracted to that.

• You may find value in writing out favored passages and keeping them around for consistent review for several days or as long as they nourish, and then come back to them again and again when attracted.

• Memorize, but more important, literally *learn by heart*. The Lord's Prayer can very quickly be committed to memory, but it takes a long time to learn by heart. Scripture texts, psalm verses, loved phrases from other sources will then rise up out of your heart and truly nourish and slowly transform you.

• Know that *lectio* is far better taught by a person in true tradition than by any number of books. Therefore, be willing and free in helping others by your own experience, both failures and successes, in coming to a practice of *lectio* that nourishes the whole life.

Father Michael Casey speaks of *lectio* and *meditatio*—both of them components of mindfulness—as "the evangelizing of our consciousness." It leads us to remember God and become what God calls us to be.

Chapter 4

Fruits of Monastic Life

*A*BBA LUCIUS ASKED SOME VISITORS about their manual work, and they said piously, "We do not touch manual work, but as the Apostle says, we pray without ceasing." The old man asked them if they didn't eat. When they replied they did, he asked, "When you are eating, who prays for you then?" And he asked them if they didn't sleep, and when they admitted they did, "Who prays for you then?" They could not find an answer. "Forgive me, but you do not act as you speak. I will show you how, while doing my manual work, I pray without interruption. I sit down with God, soaking my reeds and plaiting my ropes, and I say, 'God, have mercy on me; according to your great goodness and according to the multitude of your mercies, save me from my sins.'" He asked them if this were not prayer, and they replied it was. Then he said to them, "So when I have spent the whole day working and praying, making thirteen pieces of money more or less, I put two pieces of money outside the door and I pay for my food with the rest of the money. He who takes the two pieces of money prays for me when I am eating and when I am sleeping; so, by the grace of God, I fulfill the precept to pray without ceasing."

Abba Lucius is witness to a number of characteristics of the early monks: simple common sense in contrast to self-regarding bogus piety, speaking the truth in love, something of that strong and good sense of taciturnity. Abba Lucius also dispels the myth that a monastic life is spent exclusively in the chapel, and challenges everyone to think of prayer in broader terms.

There are somewhat less measured and more astringent sayings of the Desert Fathers, like that of Theodore of Pherme, who anticipated some later generations in saying, "In these days many take their rest before God gives it to them." There doesn't seem to be a great deal of that among the early monks; there does seem to be a real regard for work accomplished in and for Christian love. We are told of Abba Serapion and his monks that "it was the custom not only among these, but almost all the Egyptian monks, to hire themselves out at harvest time as harvesters, and each one among them would earn eighty measures of corn, more or less, and offer the greater part of it to the poor, so that not only were the hungry folk of that countryside fed, but ships were sent to Alexandria, laden with corn, to be divided among such as were prisoners in gaols, or as were foreigners and in need. For there was not poverty enough in Egypt to consume the fruit of their compassion and their lavishness."

The work of these monks was surely transformed by the whole perspective of service in which it was accomplished. The use of the term "service" rather than "work" might change our perception in many ways and obviate some of the difficulties we have associated with work.

SERVICE, MOTIVATED BY LOVE

To be asked simply to work may, rightly or wrongly, sometimes seem exploitative; to be asked sincerely to serve puts it in quite another context. Service is other-regarding; I am much less likely to be focusing on my work in any possessive sort of way. I am less likely to become that bogey of recent years, the workaholic, and more likely to realize that I must provide the prayer and the leisure and the *lectio*. I must have a balanced life so there is a "well," a "fountain" out of which genuine service can flow.

In the light of the early monastic sources and especially the Rule of Benedict, substituting service for work in our conversation is not arbitrary.

Benedict does speak about work somewhat negatively, as a sort of "remedy for sin," when he says, "Idleness is the enemy of the soul. Therefore, the brothers should have specified periods for manual labor" (48:1). However, he surely speaks very positively too: "When they live by the labor of their hands, as our fathers and the apostles did, then they are really monks" (48:8). And he calls the monastery God's workshop (4:78) and says the monks are God's workmen (Prologue 14). And he uses "serve" and "minister" as equivalents of "work."

Work Transformed to Service

Benedict calls the monastery "a school for the Lord's service" (Prologue 45); by that very fact it is a school of mutual service. The simple statement of chapter 35, right at the outset, "The brothers should serve one another," is nuanced and applied all through the Rule: "At mealtime, they may serve their brothers without grumbling" (35:13); "Care of the sick must rank above and before all else, so that they may truly be served as Christ" (36:1); and it is all summed up in "Let all the rest serve one another in love" (35:6). Anyone who needs help is to be given it—the guest master, the porter, the kitchen servers—and almost always Benedict says this is to be done so they may serve better, not just to get the work done. The Work of God, what we call the Liturgy of the Hours, is considered service. The care of guests is service. And the motivating force throughout is manifestly love—a reverent love for God and a reverent love for human beings who are God's redeemed image.

There is, latent but real, a deep love of the human here—a loving care of bodies, minds, and spirits. Perhaps it is the root of the whole humanistic tradition in the Benedictine Order—the regard not only for human beings themselves but also for their works of spirit, mind, hands, education, the arts, craftsmanship, science, the cultivation of the soil. And because we are made in God's image and have been redeemed, a love of the human is love of God.

The root of Benedict's spirit of service is the Servant Christ. He who is Lord and Master is among his disciples as one who serves, demonstrated when he gave the most menial of services, the washing of feet. He tells his disciples he does it as an example of what they are to do. Those who are his servants he makes his friends and children of his Father. And he said that what is done to others in his name is done to him, and what services are denied to others are denied to him.

In our own time the ecclesial accent has come to be on the servant church. On one level we say rather glibly that we are the church, but at least some of the time some of us find it hard to be servant church. And yet all through the ages between Jesus' washing of the feet and post–Vatican II emphasis on the servant church, service in love has been a mark of Christian holiness. One thinks of Catherine of Genoa and her astonishing service during the plague, of God saying to that other Italian, Catherine of Siena, "The service you cannot render me you must do for your neighbors." The number of examples is overwhelming. One of today's saints, Teresa of Calcutta, has said: "In Holy Communion we have Christ under the appearance of Bread. In our work we find him under the appearance of flesh and blood. It is the same Christ."

Benedict finds a place in this history. The Rule stresses service to one another in the community. So, for the most part, do the rules of the Pachomian communities. The nature of the life for which both monastic Fathers wrote, an enclosed community, would dictate this. The possibility of a monastery's becoming corporately self-centered, ingrown, is always there. But, like the Desert Fathers, in the life of Benedict, in the various Lives of Pachomius, and in the history of their followers, there was, and is, a great deal of service in the church and in the world at large. We need only reflect for a moment on Gregory's account of Benedict's service to the shepherds around Subiaco and to the pagans around Monte Cassino.

Many monasteries in the United States today are responsible for a great deal of service. It would be a complete inversion of Benedict's Rule to stress only the extra-monastic service, the educational, the pastoral, ecumenical, cultural work and the many other activities of so many sorts in which monastic communities are engaged. Rather, would it not be true to say that the spring of all these, and ultimately the human measure of their success, is how willingly, how lovingly, and how well they serve one another in community? Any person who has lived monastic life for any length of time knows something of the cost of that service, as well as the joys, both of giving and of receiving the loving service of others.

Closely allied to giving and receiving the service of love in the community is the matter of gratitude and its expression. One of the dangers in community life can be taking such service for granted. It is not so much a question of being ungrateful as it is of failing to let the other person know we are grateful. Yet thanksgiving is so deep a reality in Christian worship and Christian life—one wonders if, when we fail to embody and express our thanks to our sisters and brothers, we ever really adequately express our thanks to God.

Hospitality, Receiving Guests into God's House

Several kinds of service seem intrinsic to monasticism, rooted in the Rule of Benedict. The first is hospitality, in the sense of service to the guests who come, in any guise, to the monastery. It may be a quite legitimate extension of the term hospitality to include education, parochial service, health care, chaplaincies, missionary service, and many other forms of ministry, but the guest at the monastery is unique.

Hospitality is a monastic virtue. Father Demetrius Dumm, OSB, suggests that hospitality may indeed be an all-embracing term for monasticism. In the Old Testament God is often portrayed as our host, for example in creation itself (giving us the world to live in and enjoy), in the Exodus journey, in Psalm 23. From God we learn hospitality—hospitality to God himself in recognizing and honoring and loving God's presence everywhere and in everyone.

Hospitality marks eremitic as well as cenobitic monasticism. Anthony in the desert came forth from his solitude to meet his guests and their needs. At first he came with some reluctance, but increasingly, as his hermit vocation deepened, so did his hospitality. A century later Abbot Cassian said:

> We came from Palestine into Egypt, to one of the Fathers. And he showed us hospitality, and we said to him, "Wherefore, in welcoming the brethren dost thou not keep the rule of fasting, as they do in Palestine?" And he made answer, "Fasting is ever with me, but I cannot keep you ever here: and though fasting be indeed useful and necessary, it is a matter of our own choosing: but love in its fullness the law of God requires at our hands. So, receiving Christ in you,

I must show you whatever things be of love, with all carefulness: but when I
have sent you away, then may I take up again the rule of fasting. The children
of the bridegroom do not fast while the bridegroom is with them, but when
he is taken from them, then shall they fast."

Benedict in his cave at Subiaco, apparently unaware of chronological
or liturgical time, did not know it was Easter until a priest appeared as
guest. When the priest told Benedict it was Easter Day, Benedict replied
that it must indeed be a great feast to have brought him a guest. And the
priest had to insist that it truly was Easter, and he was not merely a figure
of Easter blessing.

Perhaps Benedict's root saying about the reception and service of
guests is his calling the monastery God's house, in chapter 53, "On the
Reception of Guests." If it is God's house, it is everyone's. And we welcome Christ to his Father's house in each guest and care for him or her
accordingly. Benedict sets down the details for this care. The guest is to
be welcomed, treated with courtesy, reverence, gentleness, and honor.
Special care is to be given those who share our faith (in accordance with
Galatians 6:10), the poor, pilgrims, and visiting monks.

Benedict's Ritual for Receiving Guests

The Rule's providing a special ritual of welcome involving the entire
community underscores the significance of receiving guests. Such a ritual
would mean fairly complete disruption of a very ordered life—and often,
since "monasteries are never without" guests (53:16).

One feature of Benedict's ritual, once experienced, leaves a deep im-
pression. I recall a weeklong visit to Mount Savior Monastery in Pine
City, New York. Old Brother Luke met me, then graciously and without
fuss led me to an icon and offered a prayer in welcome, asking God's
blessing on my days in the monastery. It was simple, unpretentious, and
since it was evident that this was done regularly, I knew immediately the
focus, the preoccupation of the community. Of course it cannot always
be done there or anywhere else, but what a way to make explicit that it is
Christ (and no less the person) who is being welcomed!

Once welcomed, guests are to be served, and it is evident in the Rule
how very seriously Benedict took this. The other side of this service is

that the community is not to be disturbed in its way of life. Guests of the monastery presumably have come to share, not to disrupt monastic life.

Characterization of Benedictines' Service as Poetic

After hospitality, the second monastic service is an amalgam that rises out of Cardinal Newman's characterization a hundred and fifty years ago of followers of Benedict as poetic in contrast to other Orders in the Church. Many Benedictines do not like the designation, dismissing it as romantic. But without trying to define precisely what he means, Newman illustrates, and I extend his illustrations.

• Benedictines inherently love the earth, and it seems to me this derives from the Rule's earthiness and reverence: all the provisions for the simple but reverent care of our human bodies and of all the material things of the monastery; reverence for persons and looking upon the utensils of the monastery as vessels of the altar. One senses here more than economy. Such reverence is at risk in our affluent society; we go against the cultural drift when we practice this reverence.

• The whole reflective *lectio-meditatio* process, sustained, creates a contemplative mentality rather than a mastering one, nourishing— as Newman would say—imagination and affection, leading to admiration, devotion, and love rather than the coldly intellectual or the merely efficient. It opens the door to contemplative life.

• Monasticism doesn't have one point of origin or center of life but many, not one experience or expression but many, and does not grow according to a pre-ordained plan but according to life and Spirit, freely, naturally, with variety, not legislated but organic.

• Newman cites what monasticism has done to cultivate and transform the earth, not merely romantically to admire it. René Dubos, Nobel Laureate in Biology, called Benedict, rather than Francis, the real patron of ecologists. Newman says the poetry of Benedictines is the poetry of hard work and hard fare, willing hearts and loving hands. One is reminded of the American naturalist, John Muir, who said, "One must labor for beauty as for bread."

In summary, I think Newman would say one of the services of Benedictines is to create and preserve the beautiful and not only the useful, to nourish the contemplative spirit and not only the mastering spirit, to love and nurture the human and the earth as divine gift. If monastics serve in love in their communities, will they not be drawn by love into truly loving service of those outside the monastery—but to a service that is harmonious with the monastic life itself and expressive of its nature and goals? In some real measure, then, will not the Body of Christ be served and the Kingdom of God furthered?

RECONCILIATION AND HEALING, BEGINNING WITH RECOGNITION THAT WE NEED IT

A quotation from the life of Aelred of Rievaulx (1109–1167), one of the most beloved abbots in history, sets the stage for consideration of the monastic community as an environment for reconciliation and healing.

> He turned the house of Rievaulx into a stronghold for the sustaining of the weak, the nourishment of the strong and whole; it was the home of piety and peace, the abode of perfect love of God and neighbor. . . . Who ever came there in his weakness and did not find a loving father in Aelred and timely comforters in the brethren? . . . Those wanderers in the world to whom no house of religion gave entrance came to Rievaulx, the mother of mercy, and found the gates open, and entered by them freely, giving thanks unto their Lord. If one of them in later days had taken it upon himself to reprove in angry commotion some silly behavior, Aelred would say, "Do not, brother, do not kill the soul for which Christ died, do not drive away our glory from this house. Remember that 'we are sojourners as were all our fathers,' and that it is the singular and supreme glory of the house of Rievaulx that above all else it teaches tolerance of the infirm and compassion with others in their necessities. And 'this is the testimony of our conscience,' that this house is a holy place because it generates for its God sons who are peacemakers. All"—he would continue—"whether weak or strong, should find in Rievaulx a haunt of peace, and there, like the fish in the broad seas, possess the welcome, happy,

spacious peace of charity. . . . The house which withholds toleration from the weak is not to be regarded as a house of religion."

Who of us is not the weak one who might come to Rievaulx? Who of us is not in need of a loving father or mother and timely supporters in our brothers or sisters? Who of us has not needed to experience toleration, not in the corrupted sense of being put up with, but the strong sense of being carried in love, borne as a woman bears a child—giving life—when our own weakness would keep us from all we would be before God and our brothers or sisters? To whom among us would Aelred never have to say, "Do not, brother or sister, do not drive away our glory from this house?" Who of us, finally, has not known forgiveness, toleration, and healing in and from the community, abbot or prioress, brothers or sisters? Who of us would be here if we had not experienced this? And who among us has not experienced that forgiveness, toleration, and healing from others at some time as an effective sign of the Lord's forgiveness and toleration and healing?

Recognition of Need Is Necessary for Reconciliation

The process of reconciliation, healing, and peace begins with recognition that I need it. This was the great motivation of the monastic fathers. Speaking of the Desert Fathers, Benedicta Ward says, with a kind of stark and awful beauty: "They are men who recognize . . . that they are broken, incomplete, and they learn to remain incomplete, with their raw edges reaching always towards the heavens." Theirs was a life of repentance—the naked realization of their own weakness and sinfulness, the willingness to confess it, the certainty that only God's gift could heal them and make them whole. Abba Sarmatas said, "I prefer a sinful man who knows he has sinned and repents, to a man who has not sinned and considers himself to be righteous."

Benedict had known temptation so severe as a young man that he very nearly left Subiaco. He encountered violence and sin in the monks of the communities he dealt with and in the priest, Florentius. One can be sure that in the increasing sensitivity to sin that is the experience of every saint, he judged himself a great sinner. He directs his monks: "Every day with tears and sighs confess your past sins to God in prayer and change from these evil ways in the future" (4:57-58). Significantly, the two preceding verses had been, "Listen readily to holy reading, and devote yourself often to prayer." He seems to assume that, being literally struck by the word of God, one's heart will be moved both by the recognition of one's sinfulness and by the love of God, and thus be brought to compunction. He ends the chapter, "Finally, never lose hope in God's mercy" (74). Not only had Benedict experienced that mercy in himself and others, he had out of his pain learned compassion, and his Rule has many evidences of it.

In his three principal references to prayer, apart from those devoted expressly to the Office, Benedict speaks of tears of compunction, compunction of heart, tears and heartfelt devotion (20:3; 49:4; 52:4). His model of the monk is the publican or tax collector (Luke 18:13) who, deeply aware of his unworthiness, simply and trustingly puts that unworthiness before God. In an age that is just recovering from too much fruitless guilt and is thus tempted to swing to great difficulty in admitting any guilt at all, review of the old monastic virtue of compunction has much to offer us.

Compunction

Compunction is neither a preoccupation with sin and guilt nor a minimizing of it, but an honest and simple recognition of myself as sinner—not in the abstract but concretely. Yet in this very heartfelt recognition of sin is a simultaneous awareness of God's desire to forgive and my own desire, my hunger for God. Compunction is the wounded heart in the process of healing: aware of sin, deeply aware of it, and equally aware that I am capable of and called to so much more, and moved by a deep desire for God. It was only in the moment when the rebellious son in the parable of Luke 15 cried "Father!" in the embrace of that loving father's acceptance that he really knew either his father or himself. That "Father!" is a prayer of compunction par excellence. It meets all Benedict's requirements for prayer in one word.

Compunction is not a self-centered obsessive sense of guilt, an endless rehearsing of my sins. There is growth in compunction according to Gregory the Great, for whom it was a specially loved virtue. In the third book of the *Dialogues* he writes:

The penitent thirsting for God feels the compunction of fear at first; later on, he experiences the compunction of love. When he considers his sins he is overcome with weeping because he fears eternal punishment. Then when this fear subsides through prolonged sorrow and penance, a feeling of security emerges from an assurance of forgiveness, and the soul begins to burn with a love for heavenly joys. Now the same person, who wept out of fear of punishment, sheds abundant tears because his entrance into the kingdom of heaven is being delayed. . . . Thus the compunction of fear, when perfect, leads the soul to the compunction of love.

This might well have been a commentary on the rebellious son who finally returned to his prodigal father.

There is a collection of sayings about brothers dismissed from their monasteries for their faults and failures, brothers who then went to the desert abbas and found compassion. Often on the word of the abbas they were accepted again. Among the best known stories is that of Abba Moses, a converted, forgiven, and merciful robber:

A brother at Scetis committed a fault. A council was called to which Abba Moses was invited, but he refused to go to it. Then the priest sent someone to say to him, "Come, for everyone is waiting for you." So he got up and went. He took a leaking jug, filled it with water and carried it with him. The others came out to meet him and said to him, "What is this, Father?" The old man said to them, "My sins run out behind me, and I do not see them, and today I am coming to judge the errors of another." When they heard that, they said no more to the brother but forgave him.

And it was said of Abba Macarius the Elder that "just as God protects the world, so Abba Macarius would cover the faults which he saw, as though he did not see them, and those which he heard, as though he did not hear them."

Inner Conversion

As they speak of repentance, compunction, and mercy, the monastic fathers are deeply concerned about reconciliation and healing. "It was said of Abba Isidore, priest of Scetis, that when anyone had a brother who was sick, or careless or irritable, and wanted to send him away, he said, 'Bring him here to me.' Then he took charge of him and by his long-suffering he cured him." Human healing, however strong and loving, was simply not enough. One of Abba Sisoes's disciples was tempted, and "the old man saw that he had given way. Standing up, he stretched his hands towards heaven, saying, 'God, whether you will, or whether you will not, I will not let you alone till you have healed him,' and immediately the brother was healed."

Benedict is no less a man of reconciliation and healing. "See how the Lord in his love shows us the way of life" (Prologue 20). The whole way that Benedict then opens to us under the Spirit's direction is a journey into deeper and deeper conversion. The whole life he envisions is a process of paschal healing; the way into life is the way into healing.

Yet Benedict makes provision for particular circumstances within this process. The Rule is the work of a realist. Benedict seems to have anticipated, even expected, all sorts of human failure, as a thoughtful reading of the Rule demonstrates. And so he deals with possible failures, but in all contexts the emphasis is not on the failing but on the healing.

How, in light of this overall character of the Rule, could chapters 23 to 30 be designated "the penal code"? Such dreadful connotation may perhaps apply to the letter of some of those chapters, but not at all to the spirit of the Rule as a whole, and certainly not to chapters 27 (The Abbot's Concern for the Excommunicated) and 28 (Those Who Refuse to Amend After Frequent Reproofs) in the midst of that so-called "penal code." Though there is surely severity, the end is not to penalize but to awaken to a state in which healing is possible.

It is all too easy for us who happen not to be stray sheep at the moment to quote texts about what the abbot or prioress and the mature brother or sister sent to support the erring member ought to do about that erring member. Benedict completes the assertion, " . . . *let love for [the monk] be reaffirmed* (2 Cor 2:8)," with the directive, "and let all pray for him" (27:4) The force of this seems to be that all are to reaffirm or intensify love and pray for that person.

And finally there is chapter 72:

This, then, is the good zeal which monks must foster with fervent love: *They should each try to be the first to show respect to the other* (Romans 12:10), supporting with the greatest patience one another's weaknesses of body or behavior, and earnestly competing in obedience to one another. No one is to pursue what he judges better for himself, but instead, what he judges better for someone else. To their fellow monks they show the pure love of brothers; to God, loving fear; to their abbot, unfeigned and humble love. Let them prefer nothing whatever to Christ, and may he bring us all together to everlasting life. (3-12)

The cumulative effect is a life of healing, of whole-making, of transformation. Saint Augustine says, "What calls for all our efforts in this life is the healing of the eyes of our hearts, with which God is to be seen." This is manifestly what Benedict was and is about.

But healing goes beyond inner conversion. One of the lives of Pachomius describes some physical healings performed through his prayers and ministrations, and then continues:

One day he sat down and spoke out to the brothers, "Do not think that bodily healings are healings; the real healings are the spiritual healings of the soul. So, if today a man who was blinded in his mind through idolatry is led to the way of the Lord, to the point of seeing plainly and of acknowledging his Creator, is that not healing and salvation for the soul and for the body before the Lord at once and forever? And if someone else is dumb from lying, not speaking the truth, but his eyes are opened for him and he walks in righteousness, again is that not a healing? And if another's hands are maimed through his idleness in following God's commandments, but his eyes are opened and he does some good, is that not a healing?"

I like to hear the parables of mercy in the gospel. They assure me of the mercy available to me. The real test is whether I am willing to be a healer, manifestly wounded but a healer, and if I will be merciful in helping others to healing.

PEACE, AN INNER PLENITUDE

Often we think of peace as the absence of discontent or quarreling or war. But the Desert Fathers make a point:

There were two elders living together in a cell, and they had never had so much as one quarrel with one another. One therefore said to the other: Come on, let us have at least one quarrel, like other men. The other said: I don't know how to start a quarrel. The first said: I will take this brick and place it here between us. Then I will say: It is mine. After that you will say: It is mine. This is what leads to a dispute and a fight. So then they placed the brick between them, one said: It is mine, and the other replied to the first: I do believe that it is mine. The first one said again: It is not yours, it is mine. So the other answered: Well then, if it is yours, take it! Thus they did not manage after all to get into a quarrel.

There is something more here than absence of quarreling—there is a positive quality, a sort of inner plentitude very different from quietism or an angry pacifism.

In Prologue 17 Benedict quotes Psalm 4: *"Let peace be your quest and aim."* In the fourth degree of humility the monk is able even under adverse conditions to peacefully embrace suffering in his heart (7:35). He asks that all be arranged "so that no one may be disquieted or distressed in the house of God" (31:19). The monk is to make peace before the sun goes down if he has been engaged in dispute with anyone (4:73). Distribution of goods is to be arranged so "all the members will be at peace" (34:5). This monastic consciousness of and commitment to peace is embodied in ritual: the Our Father, the kiss of peace at the Eucharist, the greeting of guests.

Pax, peace, is a Benedictine motto. How can we help make our community really a home and a nurturing place of peace? Perhaps no modern cause is so native to followers of Benedict as the peace movement. Thomas Merton, deeply concerned with peace issues at the time of the Vietnam War, wrote in words of great wisdom for everyone:

> Douglas Steere remarks very perceptively that there is a pervasive form of contemporary violence to which the idealist fighting for peace by nonviolent methods most easily succumbs: activism and overwork. The rush and pressure of modern life are a form, perhaps the most common form, of its innate violence. To allow oneself to be carried away by a multitude of conflicting concerns, to surrender to too many demands, to commit oneself to too many projects, to want to help everyone in everything is to succumb to violence. More than that, it is cooperation in violence. The frenzy of the activist neutralizes his work for peace. It destroys his own inner capacity for peace. It destroys the fruitfulness of his own work, because it kills the root of inner wisdom which makes work fruitful.

The fruits of monastic life are many; perhaps nothing sums them up better than that winsome line in the story from the desert: "Thus they did not manage after all to get into a quarrel."

Desert Spirituality

Chapter 5

The Desert: Place of Meeting

ESERT SPIRITUALITY: Silence, Solitude, Simplicity. This may sound forbidding. However, something very significant about our time in Christian history is the current interest in silence, solitude, and simplicity.

Mark's Gospel recalls Jesus' forty days in the desert and calls us to enter our deepest being and open our hearts to God's transforming action in us—to conversion. Our roots are deep in desert soil.

But before we review those roots, we need a descriptive definition of the terms "spirituality" and "desert." We need to reflect on the nature of desert spirituality as the Bible—the word of God—presents it, give some consideration to desert spirituality in our lives today, and examine how a life of prayer flows out of and integrates this spirituality. Desert spirituality is not only for some special groups of Christians.

Starkness and Loneliness of the Desert

Spirituality is not simply the way we pray, any ascetic practices we might adopt, or any prayer or Bible study group we may belong to. Spirituality is essentially our being-before-God and how this works out in all aspects of our lives: our self-understanding, our values, our relationships, our commitments, our prayer, our work, our leisure, our goals and the means we use to achieve them. And when we speak of desert, we may refer either to the reality or to the symbol. As reality, as geographic place, the desert may be the dunes of the Sahara, the forbidding rock of the Sinai Peninsula and parts of the Holy Land, or much of the Southwest of the United States. The Bible calls it almost interchangeably "desert" and "wilderness" or, in the gospels, "lonely place."

Though people can come to love the geographic desert, it is no place to get romantic about. Neither, as we shall see, is desert spirituality. An American lover of the desert—Edward Abbey, who has been called the Thoreau of the American West—writes:

> The desert says nothing. Completely passive, acted upon but never acting, the desert lies there like the bare skeleton of Being, spare, sparse, austere, utterly worthless, inviting not love but contemplation. . . .
>
> Despite its clarity and simplicity, however, the desert wears at the same time, paradoxically, a veil of mystery. Motionless and silent it evokes in us an elusive hint of something unknown, unknowable, about to be revealed. . . .
>
> The desert waits, . . . desolate and still and strange, unfamiliar and often grotesque in its forms and colors, inhabited by rare, furtive creatures of incredible hardiness and cunning, sparingly colonized by weird mutants from the plant kingdom, most of them as spiny, thorny, stunted and twisted as they are tenacious. . . .
>
> Even after years of intimate contact and search this quality of strangeness in the desert remains undiminished.

Others are much harsher in their judgment and call the desert evil. At best it demands being taken very seriously. The desert can be beautiful, but it is an austere beauty; it can be a setting for deepened, renewed inner life, but it can as easily be life-threatening. The desert demands decisions, choices, and we have to make the right ones or our lives are in danger. There is no place for the trivial, the unnecessary, preoccupation with comfort. We are stripped down to essentials.

It's sometime in the 1950s, I'm watching a storm come to the boil. The wind rises sharply, the light changes, the trees are lashed and the clouds a turbulence. In the midst of this a red-tailed hawk breasts the wind just to the south, riding the turbulence with quiet wings, exultant in facing the storm as it gathers force, threatens to break in full fury. Just before the slashing rain it disappears into the growing darkness.

—*Grace Notes*

STORM HOVER

*R*iding the roil of the wind,
a hawk crests the surge and the slack
of the storm
with no beating of wings.
 And shall I not learn
  so to greet and not buffet the gale?

—*Grace Notes*

The sun blazes by day, nights become numbingly cold, and you can soon get dehydrated. You can die of thirst or be swept away by sudden torrential rain. There are venomous snakes and sometimes dangerous wild animals. In brief, in the desert we are terribly vulnerable.

Incredible Beauty of the Desert

But this is not the whole picture. The desert blooms. When all the forces of nature come together in the right balance—sun and moisture and temperature—the desert flowers into dazzling beauty. We can't arrange for it, and we can't foretell it precisely; but when the time is right, there is a burst of life and beauty all the more awesome for its stark setting. Anyone who has seen a desolate desert terrain transformed into vast stretches of delicate and beautiful flowers knows the other side of the desert mystery. Isaiah (35:1-2, 6-7) saw it:

> The wilderness and the dry land shall be glad,
>   the desert shall rejoice and blossom;
> like the crocus it shall blossom abundantly,
>   and rejoice with joy and singing. . . .
> For waters shall break forth in the wilderness,
>   and streams in the desert;
> the burning sand shall become a pool,
>   and the thirsty ground springs of water.

Exploring the Spiritual Desert

So much for the geographic desert, the so-called "real" desert. Everything we have said of it is symbolic of the spiritual desert. The desert we sometimes experience within is stark, harsh, empty, often desolate, apparently unfruitful. It is mysterious, not subject to our control. Some would call it an evil state. It is threatening. It calls for some basic courageous decisions, and it has little place for the trivial, the unnecessary. It will not, any more than the geographic desert, tolerate preoccupation with self-indulgence and the search for comfort. There are storms and long nights. And in this inner desert, too, we are terribly vulnerable.

Yet, as Edward Abbey said of the geographic desert, "it evokes in us an elusive hint of something unknown, unknowable, about to be revealed." And, like the geographic desert, the inner desert can suddenly blossom. I can't program it, and I can't forecast it precisely, but when God's wisdom and love see that the character and quality and events and responses of my life are in some vital order, there is an unaccountable burst of life—a clarity, a new vision, a depth of trust, a new capacity for love, a perception of truth, a previously unknown relation to God and others. My desert blooms, and again it is all the more beautiful in contrast to the desolation I had known before. The truth of all this can best be seen in the desert experience in Scripture.

Old Testament Desert Dwellers

So many of the great figures of faith in the Old Testament were led or sent into the desert, there to experience God's love and God's lordship, often painful purification, and finally blessed transformation from the divine hand. Theirs was profound experience of desert spirituality, archetypal and instructive for us as we face our desert.

First in the long line was Abraham. At God's directive, Abram left the flourishing urban community of Haran and went out into the desert, trusting the God of promises to show him the way and the destination, and trusting that God's promise of descendants would be fulfilled. We know the story but perhaps have not paused over that mysterious sentence in Genesis 15:12 about the sealing of the covenant, a sentence noted already in the first chapter of this book: "As the sun was going down, a deep sleep fell upon Abram, and a deep and terrifying darkness descended upon him." This suggests the inner desert with which Abraham must have lived for much of his long life. But we know that Abraham did have the promised son and a whole nation of heirs according to God's promise.

Of course, the most important Old Testament desert figure is Moses, and with him the people who are our forebears in faith. Born in an alien desert land where his people were enslaved, Moses as a young man fled to the desert of Midian after killing a murderous Egyptian. While pasturing his father-in-law's sheep in that desert, Moses saw a bush burning that was not consumed. God spoke to him out of the flaming bush: "I am the God of your father, the God of Abraham, the God of Isaac, and the God of Jacob. . . . I have observed the misery of my people who are in Egypt" (Exodus 3:6-7). And God sent Moses, in spite of his justifiable fears and abundant objections, to tell Pharaoh to let his people go, and then to lead that people to a land of promise.

Moses and his brother Aaron told the king of Egypt that the God of the Hebrews had encountered them in the desert and asked that the people be allowed to go on a three-day journey into the desert to sacrifice to their God. Pharaoh, as we know, refused and made the condition of the Israelites even worse than before.

But the Lord had not only commissioned Moses; he had given him the power needed to carry out that commission. And so the ten plagues. The night of the tenth plague, the death of all Egypt's first-born, was the night of the Passover. In the darkness the Israelites were freed to go into the desert, and Scripture says that the Lord kept vigil that night (Exodus 12:42).

Then began forty years of desert life for Moses and the Israelites. There they were to trust in God and in God's word, in God's providing for their needs, in the real freedom God secured for them, and in the ultimate realization of a promised land. But we know the Hebrews lost faith to the point of apostasy and idolatry in the desert. They complained about hunger and thirst, and then about the food and the water. They had wanted freedom from slavery, but slavery in Egypt had had its own comforts compared to this desert freedom. They railed at the Lord and Moses for getting them into this challenging, demanding freedom; they wanted to go back to Egypt and slavery. And they obviously lost faith in the promise.

While the people vacillated, failing in faith and obedience, wanting life on their own terms and on their schedule for progress, Moses simply wanted God. He had left everything to do God's will and to seek God's face. He had encountered many perils in the process. He had some signs, surely, of God's presence and fidelity even in the aridity and darkness of the desert. But there are mirages in the desert, and Moses had to struggle for faith and hope. He was tried and purified. Finally, when Moses had, through both his fidelity and his failure, through the pain of trying to be faithful while the people complained and rebelled and lost faith—when

Moses had become quite totally open to God and quite totally emptied of his ego self—he met the Lord, on Sinai, in the most austere of desert land. God there renewed the covenant, revealed his Name, and gave the Law, which was to be a loving presence of God guiding his people until the New Covenant and the New Law.

The description of God's self-revelation to Moses in Exodus 34:6-7 is exquisite: "The LORD passed before him, and proclaimed, 'The LORD, the LORD, a God merciful and gracious, / slow to anger, and abounding in steadfast love and faithfulness, keeping steadfast love for the / thousandth generation, forgiving iniquity and transgression and sin.'" And now Moses, in contrast to his first meeting at the burning bush, does not focus on himself, his misgivings, concerns, fears. Moses now asks simply for blessings for the people: "If now I have found favor in your sight, O Lord, I pray, let the Lord go with us. Although this is a stiff-necked people, pardon our iniquity and our sin, and take us for your inheritance" (34:9).

Then Moses went down the mountain, his face so radiant the people were in awe and could not look at him directly.

Ultimately, not only Moses but the people as well were transformed by the desert experience. Under Moses' leadership, God forged a people in that desert. They had come out of Egypt a fragmented aggregation whose forebears and relatives had been enslaved for several hundred years. Through successive testings, challenges, purifications, demonstrations of the Lord's care, they finally became a people with their own land, their own worship, their own culture, and their own sacred history.

Our Personal Response to Desert Experience

This desert story of Moses and his people seems familiar. When God asks something difficult of us, as of Moses at the burning bush, we multiply misgivings and excuses. When we are asked to face the alien forces of our own time and place with fidelity to God's message, we seek a way around it. Especially when we are told to go into the forbidding desert and trust totally to God's showing us the way in process, told to believe that God will really meet all our genuine needs and will finally lead us to fulfillment—don't we waver? When we are called on to give up the little spurious comforts of a very materialistic civilization that has enslaved us to some degree or other and are called into the values of desert freedom—don't we rebel? We even rebel sometimes to the point of idolatry—fashioning little gods out of our pitiful grasping at power, our material baubles, our petty ambitions, and all the rest of our hoard of suspect treasures. I want to progress on the route through the desert that I determine. I want to be in command, so that if and when I arrive I can say it has been my accomplishment, that I have the mastery.

Then don't I need to be tested in the desert, challenged, purified, to become aware of my frailty and God's strength, of my infidelity and God's unending faithfulness, to be healed of my enslavements and set free at the heart of my being, to learn to trust deeply in the God of promises? I need to learn not to try to program God, but to believe in divine love, the divine will and capacity to care—I need to rely on it and accept it as gift. I need to leave it to God to choose the time and place where, like the purified Moses, I meet God and come to know divine love in direct communication. Must I not, like Moses, ultimately come to God healed of my radical self-centeredness, and with deep compassion for others and concern for their needs?

The desert story goes on through the lives of many others in the Old Testament and then in the New. But, lest desert spirituality seem not only threatening but even repellent, tempting us to run from it, a couple of very important observations need to be made.

Journey to Intimacy with God

First, the desert, in this biblical and spiritual sense, is never a place to stay. It is a situation to *go through*. You don't settle in there, you journey on and out. And you come to a land of promise, as Moses did in being on the mountain for forty days with the Lord he had longed for, and as the people did in coming to the land beyond the Jordan. In this life it is never the fullness of being with the Lord, never the fullness of the final Promised Land. But all through biblical and Christian history we have vibrant example after example of people who have made the hard journey through their desert and come, even in this life, to undreamed of intimacy with God and a land of promise in which that intimacy overflows into all aspects of life.

Others may not recognize it, but the person who experiences it knows. So—the desert is for the Promised Land.

In good old biblical language, "the second is like unto this" (see Matthew 22:38)! In Christian faith and life, the seemingly or really negative aspect is always for the positive. Not only is the desert for the Promised Land, but Lent is for Easter; death is for more life, as Christ's death was; discipline is for strength and vitality; real obedience is for real freedom; ego-emptying is for receptivity and space that God may fill with divine life. And looking ahead to the next chapters, silence is for the word, solitude is for communion, and simplicity of life is for deep riches.

With these observations in mind, and as further illustration of their truth, let us rapidly survey the experience of other significant desert figures in the Old Testament. God told the prophet Elijah to leave the city of Tishbe in Gilead, go out into the desert, and trust to God's care for him (see 1 Kings 17–19). God's care did not save him from persecution at the hands of the wretched queen Jezebel, the pain of paganizing influences among his people, fear for his life, and deep darkness of spirit. But God nourished Elijah for his journey through the desert until he too had a profound experience of God's presence on the mountain—but an experience uniquely his own, and in some ways contrasting with the experience of Moses. What they shared was that both sought God, not primarily God's gifts, and God gave them the greatest of gifts—himself.

Because the Israelites, having come into the land promised to them, became permeated with the values of their surrounding cultures—as has so often happened to God's people throughout history, saturated especially with degenerate and conflicting values, beliefs, and practices—the prophets after Elijah had constantly to remind their generations of what God had done to and for his people in the wilderness, purifying them on the desert journey from Egypt to Canaan.

The prophets, like the book of Deuteronomy, portray those desert years as the time of ideal relationship between the Lord and his people. Then God cared for them, formed them, taught them, parented them in love, preparing them for the fullness of life, opening them to faithful love.

This idealization of the desert experience is a theme in Jeremiah as well. In a period of Israel's infidelity, Jeremiah wrote:

The word of the LORD came to me, saying: Go and proclaim in the hearing of
Jerusalem, Thus says the LORD:

I remember the devotion of your youth,
    your love as a bride,
how you followed me in the wilderness,
    in a land not sown.
Israel was holy to the LORD;
    the first fruits of his harvest. (Jeremiah 2:1-3)

But Jeremiah had a desert experience of his own. His call to prophesy was
one long desert experience, and sometimes the pain burst from him in
near-rebellion.

Hosea's own experience of his wife's infidelity becomes a powerful
symbol of Israel's unfaithfulness to God.

I will now allure her,
    and bring her into the wilderness,
    and speak tenderly to her. . . .
There she shall respond as in the
    days of her youth,
as at the time when she came
    out of the land of Egypt. (Hosea 2:14-15)

And Hosea continues, saying that when Israel does return to the Lord, he
will say: "I will take you for my wife forever; I will take you for my wife in
righteousness and in justice, in steadfast love, and in mercy. I will take you
for my wife in faithfulness, and you shall know the LORD" (Hosea 2:19-20).
"Know the LORD" here has its rich biblical sense of marital love and intimacy, as, most famously, in Adam "knew his wife, Eve" (Genesis 4:1).

And then there is Job. He loses everyone dear to him and everything
that had given him "position" among his people. He is made a pariah, a
reject, by his loathsome sickness. God is silent. His friends don't understand a thing. But, finally in total surrender, Job comes to know God, and
his desert blossoms as never before.

The desert doesn't end with the Old Testament. John the Baptist "became strong in spirit, and he was in the wilderness until the day he appeared
publicly to Israel" (Luke 1:80), and "the word of God came to John son of
Zechariah in the wilderness" (Luke 3:2). Schooled by God in the desert,

John left the desert to do God's work, and recognized the Lamb of God, pointed his own disciples beyond himself to Christ, chose to decrease that Christ might increase. Jesus accepted baptism at this desert man's hands, then went to the desert himself, and began his public ministry only when John was taken from the final desert of his prison and beheaded.

Desert Experience of Jesus

Exploration of the spiritual desert comes to a climax in Jesus. Luke says that when Jesus was praying at the time of his baptism, the Holy Spirit came upon him (3:22). Then, full of the Holy Spirit, he was led by that Spirit into the desert (4:1-2). Mark says the Spirit drove Jesus into the desert (1:12). There he remained forty days, reflecting the forty years of Israel's desert experience. Like Moses on Sinai, he fasts for forty days and forty nights. Like Israel, he is tempted in the desert—tempted to put bread, material things, immediate satisfaction in first place; tempted to choose power and dominion as the way of his mission rather than accepting the role of Suffering Servant from his Father; tempted to test the Father's word rather than trust it. There are deep resonances here with the desert temptation of Israel, and Jesus responds to Satan from the very chapters of Deuteronomy that tell of Israel's desert testing: he affirms that he will live by the word of God, serve God alone, and not question the Father's promises.

A fifth-century bishop of Lyons, Eucherius, wrote: "And the new Adam drove off the seducer of the old Adam. What a triumph for the desert, that the devil who was victorious in paradise should be vanquished in a wasteland!"

After the temptation, in the power of the Spirit, Jesus returns to Galilee and begins a totally committed, immensely effective ministry. Frequently during this ministry, the gospels tell us, he chooses to go to the desert, not to be tempted but to pray, to rededicate himself to the way of life that had been clarified for him in the desert trial, and to be wholly, undistractedly present to the Father. Ultimately his way of life and his ministry bring him to his final desert: the whole sequence beginning in the Garden of Gethsemane, climaxing on Golgotha, but moving on to the total transformation, resurrected life on Easter Sunday—transformation of desert into paradise, ultimate promised land, not only for Jesus but for us.

Choosing the Desert

In our turn we can, like Jesus, either be led into the desert to be tested or choose to spend some desert time in prayer, in total openness to God.

When we are led (or driven!) into our own deserts—whether they be the death of a loved one, spiritual emptiness and darkness, illness or the long demanding care of someone else who is ill, the fracturing of a trusted relationship, a seemingly absent God, our own failures, a difficult marriage or painful fidelity to a religious vocation, the loneliness of being a widow, the loss of material goods and security for family, a prolonged struggle to surrender wholly to God, prolonged separation from someone we love, frustration of cherished hopes—whatever our desert may be, the word of God and the experience of Christian history are there to help us refocus our vision, trust the journey, believe in the God of life and love who journeys with us through the desert and welcomes us into more life and deeper love after each desert journey, and into fullness after the last journey.

Meanwhile we can, like Jesus, choose the desert from time to time—for Lent, for retreat, for regular times of prayer. Then we deliberately allow ourselves to be led, taught, formed, and transformed as God wanted to do with the Israelites, that we might know, love, trust the Lord utterly.

Finally, whether we are in the desert of temptation or the desert of choice, Jesus himself gives us the living water of baptism by which we are empowered to live ever more deeply, and bread from heaven in the Eucharist to nourish his life in us. He is our way through our deserts and into the promise, a promise he made when he said, "I came that they may have life, and have it abundantly" (John 10:10).

Chapter 6

Silence and the Word

HE DESERT IS SILENT. It can be a frightening silence, but to those who know the desert deeply, it is a kind of vast, peaceful, embracing silence. By contrast, we today are inundated with sound. We are overwhelmed with words—printed words, spoken words, painted words, neon words—these words! Then we are so often assaulted with noise, seemingly interminable noise around us, from the ceaseless rumble on the Interstate to the noise we needlessly, mindlessly make with everything from dishes to desk drawers; noise in walking, talking, and the simplest movements in our day. There is often a kind of violence in our noisiness that might reveal to us our unquiet depths. Finally there is that noise within—the endless, busy dialogue we carry on in our own minds, a dialogue that may surprise us when we reflect on it in silence.

We need to be clear what silence is not. In the first place, silence is not just an absence of speech or sound or noise, any more than peace is merely an absence of conflict. Silence has its own being, its own reality, its own richness, its own presence, and its own nurturing power. True silence is an affirmation, not a negation, and is the precondition, as noted earlier, of true reverence for speech. Just as there is "a time to speak," there is also "a time to be silent" (Ecclesiastes 3:7).

Second, true silence is not to be confused with its counterfeits, its deformations. Most have known at some time or other the destructive silence of someone's bitter refusal to communicate—the so-called "silent treatment." Further, we have known, by either observation or experience, the silence that simply cuts another off in disdain, rejection. And we have experienced silence that is merely empty, nervous, useless.

Third, silence is not an end in itself. Exterior silence is for interior quiet, and both aspects of silence are for the word, all dimensions of the word. The word—whether it be the divine Word, human words, the word of the indwelling Spirit in our own hearts, or "the word" in the sense of communication in the arts or the created world—the word has its origin in silence. It can only be heard in silence, and if it is to be effective and fruitful, it must rest in that receptive silence and be nurtured to maturity there.

What, then, is real silence? It is a positive receptivity, a creative waiting, a welcoming openness. It is openness to God, to our deepest selves, to others, both as individual persons and as the human community, to beauty and truth and goodness, to mystery—and to the word of Scripture that reveals God, and to the Word who is God's Son. The word that brought the created world into being was spoken out of the creative silence of God. Scripture is full of the call to "Hear the word of the Lord!" And the daily prayer of Jews today, the Shema, begins with that ringing call from Deuteronomy: "Hear, O Israel!"

If we are to hear, truly and deeply, we must be silent enough to really listen. "But I have calmed and quieted my soul, like a weaned child with its mother; my soul is like a weaned child that is with me" (Psalm 131:2). "In returning and rest you shall be saved; in quietness and in trust shall be your strength" (Isaiah 30:15).

Silence Becomes Prayer

In the New Testament, Zechariah doubts God's word that a son will be given in his and Elizabeth's old age, the desert of their long years of waiting. As a consequence of his doubting that word, the power of speaking words is taken from him. But after a desert time, a nine-month retreat in silence, the desert blooms—Zechariah speaks profoundly. Luke attributes more consecutive spoken words to him than are credited, in all the gospels, to any other person except Jesus himself. Among Zechariah's words is the prayer, the *Benedictus*, included every morning in the Liturgy of the Hours. Then the word of the Lord came to Zechariah and Elizabeth's son John in the silence of the desert. Out of that silence he prepared the way for Jesus and was himself prepared to recognize the Lamb of God when he came among us (see Luke 1:5-80).

The liturgy of Christmas uses this text from the Book of Wisdom (18:14-15): "For while gentle silence enveloped all things, and night in its swift course was now half gone, your all-powerful word leaped from heaven, from the royal throne." We are told that Mary pondered the word in the silence of her heart (Luke 2:51), and obviously the beloved disciple listened deeply, in the silence of a quiet heart, to the Word who was God. In the silence of the desert Jesus prayed, in the silence of Gethsemane he gave himself to his Father's will. Jesus was majestically silent before the worldly man who put him on trial and to torture, accepted the silence of his Father on Golgotha, and in the silence of Easter morning conquered the silence of death.

Should we not then learn to receive and respond in silence to this God, the Word who is God's Son, and to God's self-revealing word in Scripture? Must we be busy with words all the time? Or do we need to learn a desert silence out of which our silence itself becomes prayer? Mother Teresa has said:

> The fruit of prayer is a deepening of faith.
> The fruit of faith is love,
> and the fruit of love is service.
> But to be able to pray we need silence; silence of the heart.
> And if we don't have that silence, we don't know how to pray.

In Silence, the Silent God Opens New Depths

So, silence is for loving receptivity and response to all the ways God chooses to be manifest to us. But silence is also a loving attentiveness and receptivity to our own true selves. It takes quiet and silence to know one's own depths, to open the successive doors to the very center of our being,

$\mathscr{Y}$ou have spoken to my heart. I only begin now to understand a little how often, how mysteriously, how deeply, how variously, how hauntingly. Often my heart was too busy to listen, too engaged elsewhere, too fearful.

—*Grace Notes*

to our "heart" in biblical language. It may be a long journey, and it may take us years to get there, but isn't that what life is given to us for—to get to the Promised Land? And quiet and silence are our guides.

At the beginning of the journey I am preoccupied with myself at the most superficial level. I call it an ego trip in others and judge it there as terribly immature, shallow narcissism; but I don't even realize when I am in that state myself. If I go a little farther into my own consciousness, I begin to recognize the ego self, the superficial self, and all its games and subterfuges. I am invited to face my self-centeredness, the unworthy motivations and petty ambitions, the little meannesses, and all the rest of the trivial and sometimes nasty thoughts and reactions and schemes. When I am willing to open that door and take a good look, I recognize a kind of "slavery in Egypt," a mindless succumbing to forces that are not truly myself, because I do not want to pay the price of freedom.

One way to open the door and get a good look at that Egypt, at those rather unlovely selves in captivity, is to be silent enough to listen to our inner dialogue, our talk to ourselves. How often do I spend inordinate amounts of time and energy rationalizing my unpleasantness to others, or rashly imputing motives to others when I really know nothing about it, scheming how to get the attention or the affirmation I want, rehearsing old or recent hurts, thinking up the smart answer I wasn't sharp enough to give in a recent conversation, or gloating over a clever remark I did manage to get off, scheming how to get what I want even if I don't really need any of it?

Opening this door is not a pleasant experience; the key is silence, and I'd rather throw it away. I want to avoid at almost any cost a real look at that stratum of my being. And hence I want distraction, excitement, noise, anything to catch and divert me from facing the threatening desert within.

But, thank God, that level is not really the depth of ourselves. If I am true to authentic silence, even in that desert of my ego, if I accept the pain and radical honesty about it and acknowledge my need, the silent God will open new depths. At first I may have only glimpses, but I come little by little—unless God chooses another timetable—to recognize my true self, that center of my being where the three-personed God indwells me as gift of baptism, where I am the image of the living, loving, creative God. I come more and more to want to live always at this heart of my being. Here I am quiet enough to hear the constant echoing of God's word and God's work, and to hear it deeply enough to let it shape me from inside out. This is no ego trip, but a coming out of Egypt to glimpse the Promised Land; this is a flowering of the desert.

Saint Ignatius of Antioch wrote that in his silence he heard the living water of baptism deep in his heart calling, "Come to the Father," and John of the Cross wrote, "The Father spoke one Word, which was his Son, and this Word he always speaks in eternal silence, and in silence must it be heard by the soul." Am I quiet enough, deep enough, silent enough to hear that living water, that one word, in my own heart?

There may be—indeed likely will be—reversions to the old unworthy inner preoccupations and dialogues, but we no longer have to look for escapes, diversions, rationalizations, excuses. We can afford now to face ourselves at that level and be honest with ourselves, and perhaps with another trusted companion on our spiritual journey. We can do so because we have seen enough to know who we really are and to accept ourselves because we know God does. We trust that the Lord is not finished with us yet and will bring us out of our ego desert into the full flowering of a God-centered life.

A person who has made this journey in the deep silence of receptivity and openness is the real inner-directed person, not only psychologically but wholly—from the heart. Such a person does not live out of compulsions any longer, but out of freedom.

And when I have made the journey to my true self, or even only glimpsed it and want to live my life from that center, I relate to others in a new way. For one thing, out of my silence I really hear their words—*hear their words*. I have to be silent to listen and inwardly quiet to be fully present to another, to hear another's word, especially if I would hear its full import. How often have I engaged in conversations where I am not really hearing the other because my own words are muscling their way into expression, and I have ears only for my own words? And if I am not attentive enough, silent enough to hear their words, I don't catch their nonverbal messages either.

This doesn't mean that my silence makes me receptive to endless empty chatter. No one I know of has been harder on the futility of chit-chat than Dag Hammarskjöld, that great human being who was Secretary General of the United Nations (1953–61). Sustained by creative silence in his very demanding service of the world, he was capable of genuine honesty, real courage, and great clarity in addressing that world, and he was ruthless on the subject of idly squandering words. He likened the incessant social talker to an egg that has been blown out—empty of life and nourishment, a mere shell. Such an egg, he says, floats well on the superficial social stream. It has no substance, is of no use or consequence—a caricature, or worse.

I think people are beginning to realize that dialogue of itself is not the total solution to our problems, whether personal or social. Those of us who talk endlessly about our personal problems seem to resolve little, keep the problems warmed over, and end up with greater and fruitless restlessness. This is not to deny that sometimes we need to speak out of our hearts when we need help. But how much of our talk about problems is really from the center of our being? How much of our endless talk is a fear or refusal to accept the desert of our own ego and traverse it in quiet until we come to our center and live our lives increasingly there?

Correspondingly, can dialogue, *simply as dialogue*, offer the solution to our communal problems, whether as family, religious community, or any other sort of group? Unless we bring some depth, some clarity, some rooted and coherent foundation to the dialogue, are we not beating the air? And it is in quiet, in some measure of fruitful reflection and prayerful silence, that we come to that depth, that clarity, that rootedness, and that cohesion. Little scraps of silence are not enough to make this fruitful; if the problems and issues are real, they need to be addressed in sustained silence.

A word here, a bit parenthetically, about a term we have worn threadbare in recent years: "sharing." How much? With whom? At what depth? For what purpose? Can we really share the depths, our center, with many? Should we? How many so-called sharing sessions result in compulsive talk—words not out of silence? And how often not a silence that really hears? Is the person who does not easily participate in such sessions really antisocial or selfish or somehow suspect? These are honest questions, words that come out of silence.

By contrast, it is true that our silence can be a gift to others. Frederick Buechner illustrates this well when describing a visit to the Episcopal Monastery of the Holy Cross in New York. "So none of my questions was answered, whatever they were. I met no one who gave me whatever help I had come for or whom I ever saw again or especially wanted to. Nothing in that sense happened. But silence happened—silence at meals, in corridors, the silence of men who for the love of God kept silent; and to some degree silence also happened in myself, silence not merely as the absence of speech but as a kind of speech itself or at least as a prelude to speech, a prelude to hearing someone or something speak out of the silence." Most likely there were monks in that monastery who thought they had failed seriously in hospitality, and for some people I suppose the silence would seem inhospitable. But to Buechner, and surely to others, the silence spoke a welcome.

The person who for me best serves as archetype of one who, out of silence, related to others with full presence, full sensitivity, and full response, is the eighteenth-century American Quaker, John Woolman. He writes in his *Journal* of being raised in a family that had profound reverence for the Word of God and went regularly to Quaker meeting, where everyone was simply as present to the Spirit of God as possible and believed that the Holy Spirit spoke out of the silence both to the gathered community and to each person there.

Hearing the word of Scripture and the inward word of the Spirit deliberately and consistently, John Woolman responded to that word by loving response to everyone he met, by peacefully working for the abolition of slavery before the movement had really begun, for greater concern for American Indians when that was indeed uncommon, by speaking quietly and persistently for seamen unjustly treated, by going to England in steerage so he would share the pain and indignities of the poor, by not writing to his beloved wife from England because of the injustices to the post boys there. His *Journal* uses words sparingly, lovingly, effectively out of his lifelong inner silence. His deserts bloomed in one of the classic religious texts of all ages.

A few brief quotations will illustrate Woolman's "words out of silence," words spoken out of his own desert. About the year 1740 he wrote:

> Being thus humbled and disciplined under the cross, my understanding became more strengthened to distinguish the pure spirit which inwardly moves upon the heart, and which taught me to wait in silence sometimes many

weeks together, until I felt that rise which prepares the creature to stand like a trumpet, through which the Lord speaks to his flock. . . .

I was taught to watch the pure opening, and to take heed lest, while I was standing to speak, my own will should get uppermost, and cause me to utter words from worldly wisdom, and depart from the channel of the true gospel ministry.

Woolman wrote this as a young man. Thirty years later, not long before he died, he wrote that he did not speak in public Quaker worship for nearly a year following a severe illness, and added:

My mind was very often in company with the oppressed slaves as I sat in meetings; and though under this dispensation I was shut up from speaking, yet the spring of the gospel ministry was many times livingly opened in me, and the Divine gift operated by abundance of weeping, in feeling the oppression of this people.

In between these two journal entries, he refers again and again to waiting in silence for words from his heart, from the indwelling Spirit. As we have noted, the Spirit who gave those words also led him to self-emptying service for others. And who is to say that his silent tears before God near the end of his life were not, ultimately, more effective for the oppressed slaves than his earlier work had been?

We need to learn the positive good of a silence that is not repressive but liberating, healing, whole-making in the very fact that it can be purgative, challenging, and sometimes very unsettling. It surely cannot be all of these things until we have lived with it long enough to have learned, as Benedict did, to "live with ourselves under the watchful eye of God," and to have begun to use our speech as a vessel of the spirit. Jean Guitton, the great French lay observer at the Second Vatican Council, put it this way:

There is a kind of silence which is a primordial element, which sustains the word and gives it room to move, as a swan glides over water. This motionless lake is the first inner requirement for a genuine listening to the word. And after listening one must let the circles of the word spread, fade away, expire in the silence. The word has its origin and its term in silence. The capacity of speaking, teaching, writing poetry or even prose is the faculty of mixing the right measure of words and silence. . . .

$\mathcal{B}$efore any of the many critics can spot us, another sister and I are off into the woods on our skis. We know just the spot to stop. We take off our skis, and sink over our hips in snow. We dig down to ground level, thinking we know what treasure we will find. But no "foreknowl-edge" could prepare us for this. Under at least three feet of snow, with all the trees seemingly lifeless around us, and everything literally "in the dead of winter," there are the hepatica plants, their lobed leaves emerald green, vibrantly alive, with a nugget of ice at the core of each plant and the bud of its full spring loveliness nestled in its heart.

—*Grace Notes*

$\mathcal{I}$n the 1950s I was reading a book loaned me by a monk friend. It was a dense thing by some Italian nun. No details stay with me but a hungry awareness of her communion with God. Nothing "happens." I see nothing, hear nothing, think nothing, remember nothing. There is simply an indescribable intensity of absorption into what I can only call the immensity of God. No detail, no possibility of "analysis." No questions. No later clarification or amplification. But it has stayed with me. I have never spoken of it and would not know how, if ever I wanted to.

—*Grace Notes*

Ultimately silence leads us to the deepest part of ourselves, where eternity touches and vivifies us, where truth whispers its wordless reality. And when the silence is broken, it is broken like the bread of Emmaus on the evening of Easter: in the same instant broken and consecrated by the word.

Silence and Creation

God created the world simply by a fruitful word: "Let there be!" That word issued from eternal silence, and we know from experience that the only proportionately adequate response to the beauty of that creation is silence, or a word, whether spoken or in poetry or in song or any other medium—a word out of silence. What do you say about an emerald green hepatica plant reaching toward blossom under three feet of snow in a Minnesota winter? What do you say about a full moon rising over the blackness of a night sky in a desert canyon? What do you say about a quiet lake in the north woods at dawn? What do you say about the desert in bloom?

Something similar can be said about the fruit of human creativity. Leopold Stokowski is supposed to have said, "A painter paints his pictures on canvas. But musicians paint their pictures on silence. We provide the music and you provide the silence." Even for one who knows little of music, the pause before the orchestra begins is a silence throbbing with life. And after the concert you can shout "Bravo!" and call the artists back for curtain calls, and the critics can analyze at length. But what word communicates the depth of the experience? And what is said of music is surely true of all the arts—each worthy creation is a word out of silence, and silence is worthy of it.

My deepest concern about silence in what Henri Nouwen has called our "wordy world" is this: I fear the erosion of the experience of mystery. When we think we must subject everything to endless verbal analysis and discuss everything exhaustively, we tend, inadvertently for the most part, to turn every such topic of discussion into a problem. And when we have talked about it a great deal, perhaps compulsively, often competitively, we tend all too easily to think we have mastered it. In that milieu we tend to turn everything into problems, to focus on problems, to seek for mastery.

There are, thank God, realities we cannot master and mysteries we dare not, for truth's sake and for the sake of our own humanity, reduce to problems by deluding ourselves that words encompass them. I think it is imperative that we, as humans and as Christians, keep alive the sense of mystery and the silence that is the deepest response to it.

By mystery I do not mean the unintelligible or the essentially baffling, an enigma that challenges solution, or the darkness of the meaningless. By mystery I mean the inexhaustibly intelligible, the endlessly alluring, the depth of reality that invites us to enter again and again, to penetrate deeper and deeper, and that rewards us, not with a terminal or even a provisional "solution," but with nourishment for our minds, our hearts, our spirits. God is mystery; the human person is mystery; love, whether marital or parental, the love of friendship, or divine love is mystery; beauty is mystery; we ourselves are mystery to ourselves.

Chapter 7

Solitude and Community

N CHAPTER 5 I CONSIDERED THE DESERT—the natural desert as symbol of our personal deserts, whether chosen or accepted; symbol of both aridity and threat, and also of the sheer gift of its blossoming time. In chapter 6 I focused on desert silence—outer silence for inner silence. Silence is not mere absence of sound, not a negation but an affirmation. Silence is for all dimensions of the word—God's word in Scripture, the word of the Spirit who dwells in us, the word out of our own depth of experience and reflection, the words of others, or the word of the arts and of the created world.

Understanding Solitude

As I noted earlier, the three ways of desert spirituality—silence, solitude, simplicity—are intrinsically related, not separable. Speaking of solitude will give rise to echoes of what has been said of silence, and both lead to reflection on simplicity. Each clarifies, nurtures, and guards the others.

As the real desert is a place of silence, so is it a place of solitude. As the silence repels or frightens some people, the solitude of vast spaces uninhabited by other human beings may well be repellent or fearsome to many. As we may be tempted to fill silence with sound as an escape from depths in ourselves and from the demands of a deepened relation with God and with others, so we may "people" our aloneness with crowds and chatter and diversions of all sorts to avoid genuine solitude. Or, in an age that has been very "groupy" as well as "wordy," we may reject the very idea of solitude because it has been misrepresented to us, or for some other reason we misjudge it.

As with silence, it is necessary to say what solitude is not. In the first place, solitude is not antisocial. The person who embraces true solitude, either at certain times or as a way of life, is not running away from, not rejecting, anyone. Rather, such a person is making room within, is preparing to welcome someone—God, others, self. It is a positive choice, appropriate to a social being, and it is for a positive goal.

Nor is true solitude isolationist, seeking to cut off relationships and influences of others, insulating oneself from the human condition of other human beings. Rather, as a multitude of examples can demonstrate, genuine solitude leads one into compassion on a deeper level.

Further, genuine solitude is not mere privacy, an elimination of intrusions so I can do my own thing. Solitude may suffer many invasions without being violated, and it is for much greater ends than my "own thing."

And true solitude is not individualistic, egocentric, seeking to assert one's own self over against others, claiming any sort of superiority. It is not about expanding the ego but about losing it in the deeper self, the true self, and thus, again, nurturing the capacity for communion with others.

It is with these and similar qualities of true solitude, realities that open us to communion as true silence opens to the word, that we will be concerned.

Vocation to Solitude

Solitude opens us to communion with God, with our deeper selves, with others, with the beautiful, and with mystery. And this is true, in some proportionate measure, whether one speaks of the person who embraces true solitude at certain times that can be set aside in a very busy life, or of the person who is able, through the gift of God and of others, to live a solitary life for extended periods.

Perhaps this is the place to say something of those who are called to a more or less permanent solitary life, hermits; and those who experience an inward need for at least temporary but regular times in solitude. And since we are talking about Christian desert spirituality, we will, obviously, be concerned here primarily about solitaries, relatively permanent or temporary, as an expression of Christian life.

After more than three centuries of all but total eclipse, hermit life is being revitalized in the Christian churches of the West. It has never declined in the East. The number of solitaries is growing significantly in Europe and the United States. Someone who wrote an article about hermits in England is now responsible to a local bishop for the way of life and concerns of hermits in the diocese—hermits, plural, in a given diocese. This is hardly comparable to the fourteenth century when, Julian of Norwich tells us, there were more than forty anchorites within her city alone; but it surely signals a change from the last few centuries. In the United States there is a periodic newsletter for hermits and a listing of those willing to give their names and addresses. Not all are willing to be identified—and this not out of selfishness or false privacy, but because each eremitic vocation is unique, and each hermit has to seek out and be true to the degree of withdrawal and hiddenness to which he or she is called.

There was no plan behind this growth and expansion of hermit life in the contemporary Christian world. In the Catholic Church the hermit has been in a kind of limbo since about the sixteenth century, and even monastic communities, not knowing their own tradition, held the hermit life in suspicion. Thomas Merton's painful struggle to be granted permission by his Cistercian community to live the solitary life is stark witness to that lost vision, misunderstanding, and suspicion. And Thomas Merton's vocation to solitude is the best known of many in this country.

If there was no plan, and not only no encouragement but frequent opposition, why then the spontaneous and surprising increase in solitary vocations in recent years? Is there any other answer than the Holy Spirit? While the church, especially the Catholic Church, focused so strongly on structure and clearly defined roles, definite authority relationships, and a clearly delineated "place in the church"—while these things were the most explicitly enunciated understanding of church, that is the structured, hierarchical, institutional church—it is understandable that there was no perceived place for the hermit life where each vocation is unique. But when, as Pope John XXIII said, the Holy Spirit was inaugurating a new Pentecost in the church that accented life and holiness as primary, and structure only in its service, then the hermit vocation could revive. When the church was recognized again primarily as a profound union, as Body of Christ and God's Holy People, not united essentially by a clearly assigned position in a structure but by unity in Christ with all the vibrant charisms for mutual service that life in Christ calls forth, then the hermit vocation could come to life again.

There is still misunderstanding among many. For those with legal and structural concerns, misunderstanding may well be allayed by the formal recognition of eremitical life in the 1983 Code of Canon Law. For others, it will be the sheer vitality of the hermit vocation, the fact that God seems to be calling increasing numbers of persons to a solitude that answers their concerns. And those who know history will remember that times of significant growth in hermit vocations have historically been times of spiritual purification in the church, a herald of profound renewal.

If all this is true of those called to more or less permanent eremitical life, what of those who experience an inward need for at least temporary but regular times of solitude? A quick look at the shelves of any religious book store bears witness to the current recognition of the need for solitude. Similarly, even a brief glance at religious cassette and CD listings reveals many that suggest times of solitude and how to make them fruitful. Or search religious publications for the listings of retreat places and opportunities, and you are struck by the number that now provide hermitages or accommodations for solitary retreats. Beyond these published notices, many people find places for solitary time and prayer simply through the recommendation of others—from people who have found an unheralded place to afford them solitude for a day every week or every month, a longer period every year, and even sometimes for an entire sabbatical.

Parenthetically, it was not always so. Again, speaking especially but not exclusively of the Catholic experience, there was about a decade and a half from the mid-1960s to the mid- or late-1970s when the retreat movement declined markedly or found expression in much dialogue, in contrived ways of getting people together to "communicate" as the basic pattern of the retreat. Now the hunger is for essential solitude. This is true for most who set aside retreat times in their lives. Two particular groups may be cited here as examples of the human need for genuine solitude: those involved in ministries and women.

In an age when there is a multitude of ministries in the churches for laity, clergy, and members of religious communities, and when there are hectic activity and endless demands, there is a great deal of burnout. Henri Nouwen is one of the best-known spiritual teachers of contemporary ministers. In books like *Reaching Out, Out of Solitude*, and *The Way of the Heart* (subtitled *Desert Spirituality and Contemporary Ministry*), he speaks of the need for regular times of solitude for effective ministry, and for the avoidance of the activist disease of exhaustion. "The goal of our life is not people. It is God. Only in him shall we find the rest we seek. It is therefore to solitude that we must return, not alone, but with all those whom we embrace through our ministry."

Many women will be familiar with Anne Morrow Lindbergh's little book, *Gift from the Sea*. It is not written in an explicitly Christian context, but surely is in harmony with the Christian call to time spent in genuine solitude. By the time of its twentieth-anniversary edition in 1970 it had reached many and still continues to do so. She speaks forthrightly and often about the need for solitude. Disagreeing with John Donne's "No Man is an Island," which we sang lustily for a number of years, she wrote from her island solitude that we are all islands—but islands in a common sea and for truth's sake we must recognize this. Woman, she says, must come of age by finding her true center alone, must find some time every day, every week, and every year to become, as she puts it, "still as the axis of a wheel in the midst of her activities."

Is not the fundamental reason for our needing this solitude the fact that we are, each of us, inescapably solitaries? Is each of us not a unique being, a one-of-a-kind image of the infinite God? Does not each of us have the experience of an incommunicable depth, an awareness that, however much we might want to do so, in pain or in longing, we cannot wholly

$\mathcal{I}$am eight or nine years old. I am on the front lawn, lying in the thick grass under the oak trees. I am looking up into the expanse of a deep blue summer sky that seems to stretch silently, motionlessly, endlessly. I have an incommunicable sense of immensity around me, and aloneness in its midst. Not loneliness, not isolation—rather, it is a defining moment, a mysterious invitation into depths, beyond horizons I do not yet know.

—*Grace Notes*

open our inmost being to another? The German poet Rainer Maria Rilke speaks of "the love that consists in this: that two solitudes protect and border and greet each other." If I will not accept my own solitude, how can I accept what I cannot escape, the solitude of my death? No matter how many loved ones are with me, humanly speaking I die alone.

And yet we are social beings. If we would live our lives truly, we are stretched, extended, called to more life by responding to both aspects of our personal mystery. The temptation in recent times has been to all but submerge the solitary in the social. Perhaps we are on the way to honoring and nurturing the life-giving integration of both aspects of our human mystery. Then indeed we would have hope of a deepened relation with God, with our own truest selves, with others, and with creation.

God Speaks in Solitude

In the first place, then, solitude opens us to God—though we know that God is always present to us. Augustine exclaimed to God: "You were more inward than my most inward part, and higher than the highest element within me." The question is this: Are we sufficiently present to God, at-home for God, within ourselves to recognize God's presence there, to welcome the Lord?

Scripture is one long story of God's speaking to persons in their solitude. Abraham receives the promise under the night sky and experiences the sealing of the covenant alone as darkness is falling (Genesis 15). Moses is shepherding alone in the desert when he receives the self-revelation of the Lord and his own commission where the bush burns unconsumed (Exodus 3). Then Moses ascends Sinai alone for further revelation and receives the commandments (Exodus 19–20; 33–34). In an account reminiscent of the burning bush and the commissioning of Moses, Joshua has a revelatory encounter before the capture of Jericho (Joshua 5). Samuel is addressed at night alone in the sanctuary (1 Samuel 3). The word of the Lord seems to have come to each of the prophets in solitude: Nathan (2 Samuel 7), Elijah (1 Kings 19), Isaiah (Isaiah 6), and Jeremiah (Jeremiah 1). Ezekiel was in a group of exiles when he was called, but he alone saw the vision (Ezekiel 1).

Similarly, God speaks to New Testament figures in solitude. Four times in the first two chapters of Matthew, God communicates with Joseph in dreams, and the Magi are counseled in a dream. At the outset of Luke's Gospel, when Zechariah is alone in the sanctuary, the angel of the Lord speaks to him about the coming birth of a son, John (Luke 1). Similarly, Mary is in apparent solitude when the angel Gabriel announces to her the birth of a son, Jesus (Luke 1). Some years later "the word of the Lord came to John in the desert" (Luke 3). And still later in the New Testament, Peter and Paul and Philip receive the Lord's messages in their solitude (see Acts 10; 1 Corinthians 12; Acts 8).

The Solitude of Jesus

But it is Jesus whose example instructs us most deeply in solitary communion with his Father. Surely the hidden years before his public life were rich in such communion. Even if one were to consider Jesus to be merely a very noble human being, his life gives ample evidence of the fruit of solitude. Immediately after his baptism he goes to the solitude of the desert for forty days. Between this event and his solitary prayer in Gethsemane, the gospels abound in revealing though often very brief statements: "In the morning, while it was still very dark, he got up and went out to a deserted place, and there he prayed" (Mark 1:35); "After he had dismissed the crowds, he went up the mountain by himself to pray. When evening came, he was there alone" (Matthew 14:23); and "he would withdraw to deserted places and pray" (Luke 5:16). The last words before Luke's account of the Passion are these: "Every day he was teaching in the temple, and at night he would go out and spend the night on the Mount of Olives, as it was called. And all the people would get up early in the morning to listen to him in the temple" (Luke 21:37-38).

In these two verses from Luke we have the full impact of solitary communion with God. The God experienced in solitude sends every Old Testament leader and prophet, through the very experience in solitude, into service, on some sort of mission to others, for others—and often at great and steep cost. This culminates in Jesus, whose communion with his Father was sustained in solitary prayer and always resulted in further self-giving to others until the ultimate self-giving in the ultimate solitude, death. We know this self-giving of Jesus is the source of our true life. Humanly speaking, Jesus died alone as we all do, but his Father, the God of Life, was with him, and through Jesus' death and Resurrection, that God of Life is with us in our solitary death.

What, then, of our own communion with God in solitude? We know from the gospels that Jesus was a deeply faithful Jew—again and again we read of his going up to Jerusalem to celebrate the great feasts in the temple, of his being faithful to synagogue observance, of his going to the temple for the regular times of prayer when he was in Jerusalem with his disciples. Communal, liturgical worship was clearly an essential aspect of his fidelity to God. When the gospels speak explicitly of Jesus' praying, it is to his solitary prayer in the hills and desert and "lonely places" that they refer.

This suggests to us, at the very least, that we dare not expect our community worship to be enough in itself to sustain a really deep and vital communion with God. Jesus tells us by way of example that we expect too much of community worship and bring too little to it if we do not complement it with solitary prayer. Do we perhaps lean too exclusively on his saying "Where two or three are gathered in my name . . . " (Matthew 18:20), when his practice supplements this with so evident a rhythm of solitary prayer? Both are needed for fully human, personal prayer. So the most significant thing about Jesus' communion with his Father is not *either* that he came to pray with others *or* that he prayed at stated times in solitude. It is both—and his whole life became prayer as a result.

Fruit of Solitude

What of the impact of solitude on the self? Some people might be tempted to sum it up in one word, "selfish." But anyone who has spent considerable time in the real life of solitude knows otherwise. If what one seeks is self-satisfaction, the last place to go is the hermitage, and that must surely be proportionately true of those who seek temporary and periodic solitude out of deep human need.

As was true when we spoke of silence, the question is this: "Which self?" Do I mean the self that is created by societal expectations, worldly ambitions, the clichés and fashions of my culture, the "in thing," and the masks I put on to be accepted and, as we say, "with it"? Is that really who I am—the superficial self, the self formed mindlessly by current and therefore very transient compulsions to be relevant, important? There is no place for those selves in the hermitage; there is nothing to nourish them and I find them antithetical to my very being. They get stripped away when solitude does its work, when they are not constantly fed and manipulated by shallow social contacts.

In the process of letting solitude do that work I come, as I did with silence, to an identity not mindlessly projected on me and mindlessly accepted, but a deeper, inward self where I follow no crowd but start to become an authentic center of being, a living out of the mystery of human personhood. And I soon find out in the process, if I haven't learned it before, that I am not self-sufficient; that, refusing to let the ephemeral and compulsive dictates of the world run my life, I have not the power to run my own life. I find myself empty, needy, full of desire for the good and holy, and incapable of coming to it on my own. Then, with God's grace, I come to the indwelling God with all my emptiness, my desire, my need, my true dependence. Thus I begin to be in communion with my true self and make the beginnings of living a really human, inner-directed Christian life.

This way is a desert—anyone who has lived in it can tell you it is so. Perhaps an inkling of that desert cost, not fully articulated, accounts for people's fear and avoidance of solitude. Thomas Merton's writings on living a genuinely solitary life express this:

> The true solitary is not called to an illusion, to the contemplation of himself as solitary. He is called to the nakedness and hunger of a more primitive and honest condition. The condition of a stranger and a wanderer on the face of the earth, who has been called out of what was familiar to him in order to seek strangely and painfully after he knows not what. . . . The solitary life is an arid, rugged purification of the heart.

And again:

> The solitary life, now that I really confront it, it is awesome, wonderful, and I see I have no strength of my own for it. Rather, I have a deep sense of my own poverty and, above all, an awareness of wrongs I have allowed in myself together with this good desire. . . . Contrary to all that is said about it, I do not see how the really solitary life can tolerate illusion or self-deception.

It seems to me that solitude rips off all the masks and all the disguises. It tolerates no lies. . . . The need to be entirely defined by a relationship with and orientation to God my Father; that is to say, a life of sonship in which all that distracts from this relationship is seen as fatuous and absurd.

It is a long journey, and one does not look for immediate or magical results. Merton knew he was called to that desert, and he would not abandon it for anything else. It is clear from his writing that right along with the pain there was happiness; in the midst of the desert aridity there are blossoms of joy. And he surely became more and more a true self, a real human being, in the process.

Balance between Solitude and Service

Finally, what of the relation, the communion with others, out of solitude? By implication at least, in saying at the outset what solitude is not— not isolation, not rejection, not mere privacy or individualism—we have already touched on this.

We noted in Scripture the pattern of God's addressing persons in solitude, seemingly always commissioning them to service of others. And we noted Jesus' withdrawing for solitude to return with renewed response to the needs of his people. Every Christian solitary, whether living in a hermitage for a long time or going to a quiet place now and again for some desert time, has to discern, with prayer, in grace, and often with the help of another, the right personal balance between solitude and service.

Often Jesus simply left the crowds; at other times he left his solitude precisely because of the needs of others. It is apparently an ongoing tension, never finally resolved in this life. But one thing can be said for certain. Persons seeking to be truly solitary are profoundly sensitive to others' needs—this out of their own scarred heart, and out of constantly renewed awareness of God's compassion in Jesus. A particular hermit may be called to rigorous and almost total solitude. Then she or he intensifies prayer for the suffering, the needy, the lonely. And what Christian can say that the prayer of such a seeker of God is not effective, not as effective as or more effective than the limited sphere of action open to most of us?

Just how open the true solitary is to others is illustrated by two stories from the fourth- and fifth-century Desert Fathers and Mothers, among the most rigorous solitaries in Christian history. One tells of a brother who came to a certain solitary to ask his help. When he was leaving he asked forgiveness for making the old man break his rule of solitude and silence. And the old man answered, "My rule is to receive thee with hospitality and send thee away in peace."

The other may be quite a challenge for both those who are solitaries and those who are not.

> We saw this man of God [Ammon] in his cell with a wall about it: a cell is easily built in those parts, ample enough, with rough bricks: he had all that was necessary within, and had himself digged a well. But there came a certain brother, anxious to be near him for his soul's health, and he went to Ammon to ask if there were a small cell vacant anywhere, in which he might live. Then said he, "I shall make inquiry: but until I find one, do thou stay here in this hermitage: I go out even now to see to it." And leaving him with all he had as well as the hermitage, he found himself a poor cell some distance away and settled himself in it, and gave up his entire hermitage and all that was in it to the unwitting brother.

> But if it happened they were many that came, anxious to be saved, the old man would bring the brethren together, all eager in helping, and build a hermitage in one day. And when one by one the number of cells was complete, those who were to dwell in them were invited to the church under colour of making a feast, and when they were busied within, each of the brethren would bring from his cell such things as were necessary, and furnish the new cells one by one, so that by this community of charity, no utensil or aught that one needs for victuals was wanting, and yet no one knew whose might be the gift. And so on their return at evening, those for whom the cells were prepared found them furnished with all that was needful, and the habitation so provided that they could see no lack.

These are no misanthropes. There is no alienation from humankind here. And they found a deeper bond with others, a deeper spirit and exercise of community than many who live all their lives with others. God uses solitude to hollow out the heart and fill it with himself—and God is love. The solitary one, whether permanently or periodically so, is taught to embrace Creator and created, to love out of a deepened center, a renewed vision, a refashioned heart.

Chapter 8

Simplicity and Inner Riches

*I*N ADDITION TO BEING A NATURAL HABITAT for silence and solitude, the desert is also a primary setting for simplicity. The very landscape is starkly simple and thus has its own striking beauty. There is no provision for the comforts and conveniences of contemporary life we are used to in our part of the world, so there is a proportionate simplifying of expectations and lifestyles. The very clarity of the air, the space, and the clear-cut features of the landscape tend to reduce the complexities of our usual lives to their rightful scale. The whole atmosphere helps get me in proper proportion and relation—humbled by the scale, opened in spirit by the stark beauty, invited to personal simplicity within and in relationships and actions. This character and impact of the natural desert is symbolic of the human desert experience—illness, loss, spiritual darkness, painful relationships, the apparent silence of God, failure, the frustration of hopes. In these, too, I am stripped down, called to get to the core of reality, urged to face life in utter simplicity.

This simplifying power of the desert is profoundly attractive to many, alien to some, and frightening to others. Ambiguity attaches to the concept of simplicity itself. We have done strange things to the very term in the

English language. The word "simple" has come to mean insignificant, trivial, intellectually deficient, lacking in good sense, silly. Indeed, something similar has happened to "silly"—it used to mean blessed, innocent, holy, without guile. Perhaps those of us attracted to the simple won't much mind being called silly. "Simplicity" hasn't fared a great deal better. Dictionaries only say what it is not, and we understand what it is only by implication—it is not complicated, embellished or elaborate, affected; not deceitful, complex, artificial; not vain, distracted, pretentious, ostentatious.

We will speak here of a consciously, deliberately chosen personal value system that reflects the positive qualities implied in those negatively stated characteristics. At the outset, let us look at some of what Scripture says about simplicity.

Call to Simplicity in the Old Testament

Sand and stars were the simple signs of God's covenant with Abraham (Genesis 15). A desert bush became the place of meeting between the Lord and Moses (Exodus 3). At the time of the Exodus, the Israelites were told to make the simplest of provisions for their desert journey into freedom (Exodus 12). When the Israelites were hungry in the desert, God sent manna for their nourishment, but they were to collect only enough for each day's need. The only time they were permitted to collect an extra supply was for each Sabbath. Those who tried to hoard for other days found that the manna spoiled and was repulsive (Exodus 16), and the manna ceased when they came into the Promised Land. God cared for their needs but not for all their wants, and they were called to simplify.

The prophets found the simplest things to be of great significance. Samuel hears a quiet voice in the night (1 Samuel 3). Elijah encounters God, not in the great crash of a desert storm but in "a sound of sheer silence" (1 Kings 19:11-12). Naaman the Syrian at first rejects as folly so simple a remedy as the prophet Elisha prescribes for his healing—washing in the Jordan (2 Kings 5). A coal from the altar of the temple cleanses Isaiah before he is sent with the holiness of God's message to the people (Isaiah 6). Jeremiah sees in the work of a village potter at the wheel a paradigm of God's work in fashioning a people (Jeremiah 18). Ezekiel ponders the homely work of the shepherd and recognizes there a type of God's nurturing, healing, and guiding care (Ezekiel 34).

These and other prophets call for simplicity, authenticity in worship of the Lord. God, they say, is sick of burnt offerings, solemn assemblies, and the din of chanting unless they come from the heart, from the simplicity and integrity of a heart that truly seeks to worship.

And if worship comes truly from such a heart, then it will of intrinsic necessity be accompanied with a loving care for others—a care that mirrors and extends God's own care. Through Isaiah, the Lord rebukes the people for their pompous fasting and tells them that the fast that would please God is "to loose the bonds of injustice . . . to let the oppressed go free." "To share your bread with the hungry, and bring the homeless poor into your house; and when you see the naked, to cover them"—is this not true fasting? (Isaiah 58:6-7).

Through Amos God rejects the external trappings of an empty formalism in worship and demands that "justice roll down like waters, and righteousness like an ever-flowing stream" (Amos 5:24). God's will regarding simplicity, the single-heartedness of worship, is made clear in familiar words of the prophet Micah: the Lord does not want sacrifices of calves and rams and oil or any other pretentious offerings, but simply, from the heart, "to do justice, and to love kindness, and to walk humbly with your God" (Micah 6:8).

The prophets here reflect the covenant teaching. "If there is among you anyone in need, a member of your community . . . , do not be hard-hearted or tight-fisted toward your needy neighbor" (Deuteronomy 15:7). And again, "You shall not withhold the wages of poor and needy laborers, whether other Israelites or aliens who reside in your land" (Deuteronomy 24:14).

Further, not only were the covenant people to be single-hearted, sincere in their worship and in caring for their brothers and sisters, but they were not to over-plant, and they were to leave the land fallow periodically to regain its fertility. The domestic animals were to be rested on the Sabbath, and wild animals were not to be disturbed unduly (Exodus 23, Leviticus 25, Deuteronomy 22). Thus human beings, each of whom is an image of God, were to act worthily in carrying out their sacred trust—

authentic love of God, resultant genuine love for their sisters and brothers, and honest stewardship of the created world put in their charge.

If one lives out those demands with as much simplicity, as much purity of heart as one can bring to them, then the Scriptures affirm just as simply that there is no need to worry, no cause for fear. Then the Lord is strength, rock of refuge, salvation. The prophets and psalms especially resonate with this direct and simple trust:

> Surely God is my salvation;
>   I will trust, and will not be afraid,
> for the LORD GOD is my
>   strength and my might;
>   he has become my salvation. (Isaiah 12:2)

> For you, O Lord, are my hope,
>   my trust, O LORD, from my youth.
> Upon you I have leaned from my birth;
>   it was you who took me from my mother's womb.
> My praise is continually of you. (Psalm 71:5-6)

Jesus Sets the Example of Simplicity

Jesus brings all this to fullness, first in his own life and then in the life he called his disciples to live in following him. As Paul says in those key lines in Philippians 2: he emptied himself, not grasping at what was rightfully his, embraced our poor and weakened human condition in love, and thus made new life possible for us.

An interior genuine simplicity, rooted in single-heartedness, an all-embracing focus on the will of God his Father, overflowed into and characterized all Jesus did. Most of his life was unknown, lived in an obscure town in a country subject to a foreign power. Even when he entered public life, Jesus did things simply, with no jockeying for position, no manipulation, no ostentation. He invited followers with no promises, healed and cured with no great showmanship, faced temptation directly with neither self-pity nor compromise, prayed simply and from his heart, spoke forthrightly to other people in authority whether they supported or opposed him, and talked simply and with great compassion to those who suffered or were in need.

Jesus taught by simple parables, used simple images. He preferred the company of plainspoken, guileless men and women; his very presence seemed to strip the veneer from people and situations and conversations. He encountered his Father and his contemporaries straight from his heart and went straight to their hearts. He possessed nothing and was possessed by nothing; in this he was an utterly free man—free for his Father and free for all to whom the Father sent him. Precisely because he was wholly dedicated to God his Father, Jesus was, as we used to say so glibly some years ago, the man for others. He carried out that mission with the simplicity of genuine love and sought to form his followers in that same love.

It is enlightening to read the New Testament from this perspective, and in the process learn something of what Jesus calls us to be—we who are not only his followers but also true members.

Jesus says forcefully that genuine disciples shouldn't be preoccupied with wanting things. In teaching them to pray, he taught them to pray for daily bread as the Lord had provided daily manna in the desert. When he sent them out to carry on his mission, they were provided with no more than the people of the Exodus setting out to cross the desert. "Do not store up for yourselves treasures on earth"—moths, rust, and thieves will take care of those (Matthew 6:19). Don't worry about food, drink, and clothing—don't be preoccupied with these—certainly not with more than is needed to live decently.

It is our life, Jesus says, that is more important than these things. And God our Father sustains life even in the birds that don't have pantries and closets and attics and basements to store or hoard things. If God provides for the wildflowers and the grasses of the fields, Jesus says, "Will he not much more clothe you—you of little faith?" (Matthew 6:30). This kind of seeking things, of focusing our lives on things, he tells the disciples, is for unbelievers (Luke 12).

This does not mean, as we well know, that Jesus had no compassion on the poor whose very condition of life all but forced (and forces) them to focus on material things—not in order to store up for the future but to sustain life now. He had compassion on the hungry multitudes, and at the outset told the disciples they should respond to their hunger and need; only when their efforts were not enough did Jesus intervene (Mark 6; Luke 9). Our heavenly Father knows and cares about real need—again, need as distinguished from want.

If we disciples today were satisfied with what we need, if we lived more simply, would there not be far fewer people hungry and cold and homeless? Gandhi, who believed that Jesus "expressed, as no other could, the spirit and will of God," puts the alternative to our greed starkly: "I know that without an intelligent return to simplicity, there is no escape from our descent to a state lower than brutality."

Jesus tells the story of the rich man who built bigger barns to hoard his wealth and said to himself, "'Soul, you have ample goods laid up for many years; relax, eat, drink, be merry!' But God said to him, 'You fool! This very night your life is being demanded of you. And the things you have prepared, whose will they be?'" (Luke 12:19-20). Richard Rohr, OSF, who has preached retreats all over this country, the developing nations, and in Europe, said in one of his conferences that in his experience he never heard anyone confess greed. What does it say? That we don't even recognize it? A smart remark widely attributed to Billy Graham makes a pretty sharp point: "I've never seen a hearse pulling a U-Haul behind it."

So Jesus asked for simplicity regarding possessions, and he asks it of us. In contrast to the rich young man who went away sorrowful, those who genuinely became Jesus' disciples seem not to have had a great deal of difficulty over material possessions. Apparently they left their boats and their nets and their counting tables and simply went out on mission with only the barest necessities.

But sometimes they were looking for something else: position and power. Surely this is not foreign to the culture in which we live, a false value to which we can all too easily succumb. But Jesus taught forcefully, by word and example, that it is totally alien to the disciple, since it is totally alien to the Master. With the awful paradox the gospel writers sometimes exercise, it is just after the third prediction of the Passion that the mother of the sons of Zebedee (Matthew 20) or those two sons themselves (Mark 10), and at the Last Supper (Luke 22) all the disciples, ask Jesus who is greatest. Jesus rebukes them, both in his person and in his words. "The kings of the Gentiles," he says, "lord it over them; and those in authority over them are called benefactors. But not so with you; rather, the greatest among you must become like the youngest, and the leader like the one who serves. For who is greater, the one who is at the table or the one who serves? Is it not the one at the table? But I am among you as one who serves" (Luke 22:25-27). In the familiar scene of the foot washing, Jesus gives a slave's service and says, "I have set you an example, that you also should do as I have done to you" (John 13:15). In the Beatitudes (Matthew 5:2-12) and in so many other words and actions of Jesus, value systems are turned upside down—a true disciple does not seek the trappings of power but the simplicity of service.

It would be a facile—and fatal—error to restrict this message to table serving and foot washing. Jesus was talking about a state of mind and heart, not a particular catalog of special services. We might rationalize ourselves out of the latter, but we cannot escape Jesus' demand that his disciples, then and now, not seek power over others, empty prestige before others, or position to manipulate others.

If it is not material things or position and power we seek, might it not be something by which we seem especially seduced in our day: self? We hear it on every side—self-identity, self-realization, self-actualization, self-discovery, self-assertion, and self-fulfillment. There is, of course, a way in which this can be deeply human, deeply Christian: to release and realize our true self, the image of God, alive with Christ's life. That would be a road to deep simplicity. But this doesn't often seem to be what the contemporary surge of self-interest is about.

When people were seeking genuine wholeness Jesus responded, as we see, for example, in the story of the two blind men, sitting by the roadside. When they called out to Jesus, the crowd rebuked them, but Jesus simply asked, "What do you want me to do for you?"—and then he healed them (Matthew 20:29-34).

I wonder if Jesus' answer to today's convoluted preoccupation with self may not lie in that awesome challenge: "If any want to become my followers, let them deny themselves and take up their cross and follow me" (Matthew 16:24). In recent years I have pondered more and more the saying of Christ in Matthew 10:39: "Those who find their life will lose it, and those who lose their life for my sake will find it." I understand it this way: Those who seek only themselves bring themselves to ruin, whereas those who bring themselves, that is, the ego self, to naught for me *discover who they are*. It was by emptying himself that the Lord came to the fullness of who he is for all eternity—the God-man, the deepest bond between the human and the divine. And it is by following the self-emptying Christ that we can come to that fullness of life for which we are destined.

The Desert Way to Simplicity

The desert way calls for utter simplicity in facing oneself, identifying one's truest self, transcending one's ego self, and responding to others and to life in general in ways and words that flow from simple depths. Here again, Jesus leads into the desert, but a desert that blossoms with truth and goodness.

A great deal of what Jesus taught about simplicity was distilled in what we might call his preferential option for the child. Jesus is not asking for infantile responses in adults; he is affirming the qualities of the true child that can mature into adulthood, qualities that characterize the genuine disciple. The child is dependent, knows and accepts it; the disciple is dependent on God and accepts this dependence in simple, grateful humility. The child lives in the present moment, neither in nostalgia or anger about the past nor in fear or impatience for the future, but now, fully present now. The child is, normally—and sometimes to the mortification of elders—frank in speech and transparent, uncomplicated in motivation. It is to such as these, rather than to the superficially learned and self-consciously clever, that Jesus says the Father wishes to reveal himself (Matthew 11:25).

Brother Roger of Taizé made a wonderful statement that distills all this. In *A Life We Never Dared Hope For*, he wrote with obvious delight: "Eleven years of friendship with Dom Helder [Câmara]! The better we know each other, the more our meetings are like those of two little children." Then one sees pictures of him with Mother Teresa that look for all the world like another meeting of children. There was a great deal of the desert in the lives of each of them, but what a flowering! And not only for them but for us.

In addition to all that we have said about Jesus and simplicity, including his preferential option for the child, there are many other aspects of simplicity that Jesus addressed in his life and in his words. Just three more, briefly:

• In his consistent criticism of "the Pharisees" of his time, Jesus called endlessly for simple honesty and directness in judgment and speech. "Let your word be 'Yes, Yes' or 'No, No'" (Matthew 5:37), is echoed in James (5:12).

• Jesus asked for simplicity in one's approach to work. He went simply about his own life's work, with no grandiose scale in mind, and no loss of vision as he progressed through success and failure. The formation of his apostles and disciples was often a seemingly thankless—and sometimes even a fruitless—effort, but he went on about it quietly and faithfully. And he left us words spoken to Martha about fretting and fussing over a lot of little things that are not really of great importance while missing the really significant (Luke 10:41-42).

• Finally, Jesus did not want a phony simplicity, some affectation to impress others. It was a genuine simplicity that he lived and that he called and calls his disciples to live. I think of the genuine simple beauty of Shaker buildings and furniture, a simplicity that expresses authentically the values and life of that community.

Examples of Lives of Simplicity

If all this talk of simplicity seems unreal, impractical, and perhaps humanly impoverishing, some references to people who sought it and lived it in the past or near-present in our country will help bring focus; and these stories may help remind us of people we know who live a simple life that is full of interior riches and reaches out in blessing to others.

I have already spoken of the eighteenth-century Quaker, John Woolman. The simplicity of his whole life is reflected in a passage about his business concerns. He had begun as a tailor. His business continued to expand into retail trade, and the future seemed open to even further development. But as the Quakers say, he "felt a stop in (his) mind."

Woolman wrote in his *Journal* that through God's mercy he had "learned to be content with a plain way of living." His family was small and, after careful consideration, he came to believe that he was not, in truth, required to get involved in the burdensome affairs of an expanding business. It had been his policy to buy and sell only useful things; he was not at ease in selling whatever primarily served vanity. As he said, he dealt in this way of business so seldom, that when he did deal in such things he was weakened as a Christian.

Selling on credit was the custom in his area at the time. He wrote: "Poor people often get in debt; when payment is expected, not having wherewith to pay, their creditors often sue for it at law. Having frequently observed occurrences of this kind, I found it good for me to advise poor people to take such goods as were most useful, and not costly."

By nature Woolman preferred merchandising to tailoring, but as being a merchant became burdensome, he prayed to do God's will in his life. He believed this prayer was answered, and his uncertainty was resolved. He gave up the preoccupations of trade, though gradually, so his customers had time to find other places for their business. Without the complications of apprentices, he resumed tailoring alone and also became a nurseryman, raising apple trees. Thus he was freed, in simplicity, to live a life of immense service to others. Judging by today's standards, we could hardly give him the usual accolade for professional achievement and economic success—but what a human being John Woolman was!

Then there is another American, of the nineteenth century, who contrasts in many ways, Henry David Thoreau. With no apparent religious motivation, he simply chose simplicity as the most deeply human way to live. His classic, *Walden,* is full of gems: "My greatest skill has been to want but little"; "A man is rich in proportion to the numbers of things which he can afford to let alone"; "I went to the woods because I wished to live deliberately, to front only the essential facts of life, and see if I could learn what it had to teach, and not, when I came to die, discover that I had not lived"; "I say, beware of all enterprises that require new clothes, and not rather a new wearer of clothes. If there is not a new man, how can the new clothes be made to fit?" There are many more, but this is as pointed as any about the human value of simplicity of life: "None can be an impartial or wise observer of human life but from the vantage ground of what *we* should call voluntary poverty."

Perhaps the greatest paradox of all regarding Thoreau is that, as I understand from a comment on public radio, *Walden* is a favorite audio-book for commuters in Los Angeles.

And then there is Dag Hammarskjöld, whom I referred to in relation to silence. In an internationally significant position, Secretary General of the United Nations, Hammarskjöld sought simplicity—simplicity of life within, mirrored in an authentically human public life. "To be free, to be able to stand up and leave everything behind—without looking back. To say *Yes*—"

One thinks of Dorothy Day and Catherine de Hueck Doherty, of so many who have chosen the stark simplicity of missionary life or Peace Corps work, of those who serve the poor and hungry and homeless, especially those who serve most deeply by sharing their very lives with them. Each of these, without doubt, knows a great deal about the inner desert of an often painful, demanding, and frequently misunderstood simplicity. But they know, too, and experientially, that the desert blooms. And their deserts bloom for us.

Chapter 9

Fruits of Desert Spirituality

*H*ow do we draw all the major aspects of desert spirituality into our becoming prayer—the fruits of desert spirituality?

Silence, Solitude, and Simplicity: Foundation for Prayer

I do not mean to imply that the term spirituality refers only to the way we pray or the amount of specific prayer in our lives. I began with a sort of home-grown descriptive definition of spirituality as "essentially our being-before-God, and how this works out in all aspects of our lives: our self-understanding, our values, our relationships, our commitments, our prayer, our work, our leisure, our goals and the means we use to achieve them." There is a profound interconnection between how we pray and how we live out our being-before-God. Silence, solitude, and simplicity deeply affect both our prayer and our life.

The desert is symbolic of our own inner deserts and our desert journeys whether brief or long, intense or moderate, and reflection on the desert can help us not only to survive but also to see the deep possibilities for enriched life in our own personal deserts. The desert is silent and elicits silence—a silence that attunes us to a new range of hearing. As we reflected on God's word to us in Scripture, we saw that God spoke to human beings out of silence and that they had to be silent in order to hear—silent externally and internally. Correspondingly, if we are to hear God's word in Scripture now, if we are to hear the word of the Holy Spirit within us, if we are really to hear the word of others, we must be silent enough to receive their words more than superficially. And if we are to hear the word out of the depths of our own spirit, we must be quiet enough to attend. Silence attunes us to all dimensions of the word.

The desert is a place of solitude and invites me to go into myself and thus to enter into the ground, the basis, of relationships. Such solitude opens in me a more profound capacity for true communion. In the Scriptures God repeatedly speaks to leaders in their solitude, preparing them for deeper communion both with God and with their people. The gospels are studded with references to Jesus' seeking solitude for communion with his Father—a solitude and communion that always seems to result in greater compassion for and service to others. It is in that solitude, which Henri Nouwen calls "the furnace of transformation," that one can come to know oneself deeply, to be freed of the dominance of the ego self and of the compulsions we unthinkingly absorb from our culture, and to be open to the true self. It is there that one comes to know the bond with others, the deep existential Christian relationship that is the true foundation of community, and that alone gives meaning to togetherness in worship and work and leisure. And thus one is called to a new reality of concern for others and service to them. Solitude, then, is the ground of communion.

The desert in its stark terrain is utterly simple, and it calls me to strip off veneers and pretensions—elimination of the unnecessary—to come to a much more profound appreciation of the gift of life and all that really sustains it. Yet again, as we refer to Scripture, it becomes apparent how God communicates life and love and meaning in very simple ways. Correspondingly, God accepts the simplest worship and rejects the ostentatious performances some would take pride in offering. Jesus lived simply and taught simplicity—simplicity regarding material things, simplicity within (that is to say, purity of heart and quiet of mind), simplicity in relation to others. Essentially he asked for the simplicity of the true child who has matured into adulthood. Thus, true simplicity enriches inner life.

In each instance—silence, solitude, simplicity—my relation to God is opened and deepened, my capacity for relation to others is expanded and enriched, and I come to much greater self-knowledge and personal freedom. Thus, as we have said so often: the desert blooms.

Openness to Transforming Love

How then do these qualities of desert spirituality nourish a prayerful life, a life of becoming prayer? Karl Rahner defined prayer very simply, very profoundly: it is "ultimately the loving response—somehow made explicit—which accepts God's will to love." So the first thing to recognize is God's initiative. It is *God's will to love*—to love us and all creation—that is the source, the foundation, the enabling of genuine prayer. Our part is acceptance, receptivity, openness to the gift of God's creative, sustaining, transforming love. That receptivity is the heart of our prayer. It will, of course, elicit some sort of specific response in us, a response that may find expression, be made explicit, in any number of ways.

From all we have said, it must be evident that silence and solitude and simplicity open new dimensions of receptivity in us. They deepen our awareness of our need for God, and for the reconciling, whole-making power of divine love as we see ever more clearly the coexistence of our own weakness and helplessness on the one hand and the strength of our desire, our hunger for God, on the other.

And not only do silence, solitude, and simplicity expand our awareness of need for God, our existential hunger for God, but they also help us recognize and accept the loving indwelling of God. What we learned intellectually about the mystery of God's living presence at the center, the heart of our own being, takes on new reality as we ponder it in silence, live with it in solitude, bring it to sustained focus in simplicity. I begin to grasp the mystery that prayer is my inmost reality—that the Persons of the Trinity who indwell me are in constant communion with me—that prayer is therefore in harmony with my own true being. And there I can, as it were, be host to that divine communion simply by active receptivity.

We are invited further into the mystery of the Body of Christ, into the awesome truth of Paul's saying, "It is no longer I who live, but it is Christ who lives in me" (Galatians 2:20). Mother Teresa said it with typical simplicity: "Allowing him to live his life in us is prayer." Moreover, as we are opened to greater awareness of our own life in the Body of Christ, we perceive the mystery of the church, "the whole Christ," in newness of vision. In our own day, this vision is especially imperative, lest we lose sight of the ecclesial mystery in our all-but-exclusive focus on ecclesial problems. If we are receptive to this mystery reality of the church, will we not pray with the church and for the church with more fidelity and more devotedness?

As silence, solitude, and simplicity do their work in me, I am enabled to see with sharper clarity a pattern of divine love and guidance in my own and others' journeys—even when those journeys hike through desert places. As these three qualities provide a context for my being healed of narcissism, ego-centeredness, false ambition, unfounded fears, and societal compulsions, I can progressively see my sisters and brothers as loved by God, loved in Christ and living in Christ, and thus caught up in my very love of God, my own life in Christ. And I am enabled, in silence, solitude, and simplicity, to perceive as never before the beauty of the created world.

Our Loving Response to God

What, then, is our loving response that manifests our receptivity to all the evidences of God's will to love? Since each of us is a unique person, a one-of-a-kind image of God, there will be distinctive accents and nuances. But in general we can surely say that there are some basic and closely interrelated attitudes of loving response.

The first attitude of loving response is obvious: *gratitude*. Scripture is an extended recall, in gratitude, of God's presence and saving love among us throughout our history. It is almost as if this is the way the sacred writers know God best—in thanksgiving. In the Old Testament, the Psalms resound with thanks. In the New Testament, it is especially Luke and Paul who speak a great deal about thanksgiving. Praise and thanks are explicitly woven throughout Luke, and this accent is heard everywhere in Paul's letters. "First, I thank my God through Jesus Christ for all of you"

(Romans 1:8). He draws leaders and people of those churches into gratitude: "Giving thanks to God the Father at all times and for everything in the name of our Lord Jesus Christ" (Ephesians 5:20). He asks that they assist him with their thanks for the grace God has given him (2 Corinthians 1:11), and hopes that in proportion as grace spreads, thanksgiving may increase (2 Corinthians 1:11; 4:15). Thanksgiving should mark our personal prayer: "Do not worry about anything, but in everything by prayer and supplication with thanksgiving let your requests be made known to God" (Philippians 4:6). And it is, of course, central to the heart of liturgical prayer, the Eucharist—the very term means "to give thanks."

To stand in gratitude, to pray expressly out of gratitude, is to pray with a quite different quality than, for instance, in our focus on prayer of petition. This is not to dismiss prayer of petition or contrition; it is only to say that even such prayer, if offered from an encompassing gratitude, is more of a loving response to God's will to love.

William Temple, Archbishop of Canterbury in the mid-twentieth century, wrote: "It is probable that in most of us the spiritual life is impoverished and stunted because we give so little place to gratitude. It is more important to thank God for blessings received than to pray for them beforehand. For that forward-looking prayer, though right as an expression of dependence upon God, is still self-centered in part . . . . But the backward-looking act of thanksgiving is quite free from this. In itself it is quite selfless. Thus it is akin to love."

Something of this perception of the quality of thanksgiving must underlie a quite unexpected and lovely observation in Julian of Norwich's *Showings*. She refers to Jesus' frequently thanking her for service to him. Thanksgiving, then, is a godly virtue, and is not called for only in relation to God—since God embraces in love all that is, our response in gratitude should also extend to all. What would be the impact on our families, our communities, our friendships, if we were truly grateful people, freely expressing our gratitude? In an age of abundance, and one in which we have come to expect instant gratification, gratitude is something we need to learn more profoundly and nurture more carefully. Is gratitude, as one basic and pervasive attitude of loving acceptance of God's will to love, perhaps learned best in the desert practices of silence, solitude, and simplicity?

A second attitude of loving response is surely *receptivity to God's word*, to Scripture, which recounts God's loving fidelity in face of recurrent human infidelity. All through Scripture we are called to "Hear the word of the Lord"—the word of life, the word of transforming love. The prophets received and proclaimed God's word to his people, preparing them for the coming of the Word made flesh. That Word made flesh, especially as he is represented to us by John's Gospel, calls us to hear and treasure and live by—actually dwell in—God's word. "If," he says, "you continue in my word, you are truly my disciples; and you will know the truth, and the truth will make you free" (John 8:31-32).

Thus, a loving receptivity to God involves a sustained and maturing receptivity to the Word of God—attentive receptivity when it is proclaimed in liturgy, collaborative receptivity when it is prayed in communal prayer, and making the word one's home in personal Scripture reading, the ancient practice of *lectio*. Such loving openness to God's word can be learned deeply in silence and solitude and a life cleared of cluttered diversions. And the reverence thus learned will extend not only to the words but to the book of Scripture itself.

Yet a third loving response obviously related to the first two is *awe and wonder* at all of God's creation. As with gratitude for God's goodness and receptivity to God's word, silence, solitude, and simplicity help to elicit and anchor holy wonder deep within us. In fact, without them it may well be difficult for us, in our time and in our culture, to cultivate genuine reverence. We tend to probe and analyze and experiment and commercialize so very much, including the human person, that awe and wonder may not easily be our natural response to the mystery and beauty of creation. We need a contemplative attitude, nurtured within ourselves, in order to transcend pseudoscientific, even exploitative contemporary approaches to our world. This contemplative attitude has been called simply "a long, loving look at the real."

How shall we develop this capacity for awe and wonder, apart from some immersion in silence and solitude so that "the real" can reach down into us? And is not the development of such an attitude a loving response to the God who brought this world, including us, into being? This attitude is reflected and nourished in Scripture, and Jesus surely gives evidence of it

INDIAN PAINT CUP

*C*haliced in snow,
this fragile fungus
warms to living water
the ice at its crimson heart.

—Grace Notes

in his regard for human life, his spontaneous use of sparrows and lilies and sheep and wheat and oil and water as signs of God's loving care. A contemplative attitude, this nurturing of our God-given capacity for reverence and awe even for the simplest things, is surely a way to savor the full range of God-given life. And it is a way to respond lovingly to all of it as gift.

A fourth response in receptivity to God's will to love, again resonating with the others, is *trust*: not merely a superficial, cheery optimism, but a mature willingness to give oneself and one's concerns over wholly to the God who has so demonstrated loving care. This is no simple matter, however, but a profound act of faith. Even when I know the scriptural record of God's fidelity, even when I know this fidelity in my own life's history, to give myself over now with no reserve demands an act from the heart. How do I activate that heart without the transforming disciplines of the desert to open it up and to support continuing fidelity in trust? Yet what deeper response can I make to another's love than trust? And is not the measure of my trust the measure of my love?

For me, the most awesome realization is that God trusts us: with God's own life within us, with divine love, with Christ's Body, the church. Knowing our failures, God also knows our capacities in grace—and trusts us.

That leads to a fifth response, again related to the others: to act out of the center of our being, to be *centered*, to seek constantly to become more truly integrated, more whole and holy. Some years ago when cities were being emptied out at their heart in the flight to the suburbs, Robert Bolt wrote: "Both socially and individually, it is with us as it is with our cities—an accelerating flight to the periphery, leaving a center which is empty when the hours of business are over." May we hope that as center cities almost everywhere are being rebuilt, we as persons and as Christians will also reinhabit our centers?

There, in the biblical meaning of the heart, God dwells and our true self dwells. Living, speaking, acting out of that center keeps us authentic and truly the image of God we were created and redeemed to be. We are not then, as Paul says, "tossed to and fro and blown about by every wind of doctrine, by people's trickery, by their craftiness in deceitful scheming." Rather, he continues, "speaking the truth in love, we must grow up in every way into him who is the head, into Christ" (Ephesians 4:14-15). The same note is sounded in Romans (12:2): "Do not be conformed to this world, but be transformed by the renewing of your minds, so that you may discern what is the will of God—what is good and acceptable and perfect." How shall we learn, with the grace of God, to live from that center, except from the disciplines of the desert that free us from the dominance of the peripheral and the fleeting, providing a context in which we can come to our true selves?

If we seek to live in that center and respond out of it to God and to others, we will be exercising two other attitudes of receptivity: *compassion for others* and *serenity within ourselves*. We have said again and again that silence and solitude and simplicity make possible a profound self-knowledge. We come to know our emptiness, our total dependence, our capacity for infidelity and failure, our weakness of every sort, and the depth of our need. The other side of this recognition is compassion for others. And Jesus made it very clear that what is done to others—in thought or action—is done to him. If we exercise the loving compassion for others that Jesus himself practiced with such utter fidelity, then surely we are accepting, identifying with his will to love.

The last response flows from the rest: *serenity, peace*. It is Jesus' own gift to us as he said at the Last Supper: "Peace I leave with you; my peace I give to you. I do not give to you as the world gives" (John 14:27). It is ours simply to receive in that center. Repeatedly his greeting was—and is—"Peace!" Again, the desert disciplines prepare us to accept this divine gift of the indwelling Lord and to live in the serenity thus rooted deeper and deeper in our hearts.

The greatest tribute to Saint Benedict I read in all the abundance of literature in 1980, the sesquimillennium of the birth of Benedict and his twin sister Saint Scholastica, was made by Patrick O'Donovan. He wrote that if one were looking for the person who most shaped the glory of the western world, one would have to pass over a whole list of famous names of kings and statesmen, generals of great armies, and world leaders. They, he said, all too often presided over the world's agonies. And he concluded: "The man, under God, who did most for its serenities was Benedict of Nursia." This, surely, is to say that Benedict accepted, in a singularly profound way, God's will to love. Since the Rule of Benedict and living tradition are specifications of the gospel, the echoes are authentic.

The Desert Blooms When Life Becomes Prayer

Silence, solitude, and simplicity open and deepen our capacity for gratitude, receptivity to the word of God, awe and reverence, trust, centeredness, compassion, serenity. None of us has likely mastered any of these capacities, but we have begun to let them master us, and maybe are well on the way. Seeking to live in these attitudes and by them, however haltingly at times, is praying. They will keep us responsive to God's presence; and prayer, in the usual sense of words or wordless communication, will rise out of our striving to live these attitudes.

So many people seem to be looking for methods and techniques of prayer. The bookstores are full of how-to books addressing that contemporary hunger for prayer. I do not wish to criticize any of this, but simply to stand beside a statement in Thomas Merton's last book, *Contemplative Prayer*. He says we should not look for methods; rather we should cultivate an attitude or a complex of attitudes that "permeate our being with love." Later in the same volume he writes: "Prayer then means yearning for the simple presence of God, for a personal understanding of his word, for knowledge of his will and for capacity to hear and obey him. It is thus something much more than uttering petitions for good things external to our own deepest concerns."

This mastery of prayer makes understanding how to pray direct and simple. It doesn't make it easy; it does make it real. And understanding prayer this way makes possible that challenge of the New Testament that has so often troubled serious Christians: "Then Jesus told them a parable about their need to pray always" (Luke 18:1); "Pray without ceasing, give thanks in all circumstances" (1 Thessalonians 5:17-18). How can we pray "always" and "without ceasing"? Many use the Jesus Prayer—Lord Jesus Christ, Son of God, have mercy on me, a sinner—and find that they waken in the morning to its continuance in them even while they slept. Some use a mantra or short form of prayer like a brief psalm verse repeated again and again—in the old monastic form of *meditatio*. Others practically live with their rosary beads.

All we suggest here, along with Merton, is that prayer can be primarily an attitude or complex of attitudes, honed and deepened and made

holy by God's grace in our desert disciplines. Some forms of more specific prayer will surely rise frequently out of this way of life; but one is
less inclined to count and measure and be concerned about the amount
of one's prayer. Rather, one simply seeks to open one's whole life to the
transforming love of God, to have one's whole life become prayer, unceasing into eternity. And thus the desert blooms!

Part III

God's Questions

Chapter 10

Where Are You?

*T*HE QUESTIONS GOD ASKS THE ISRAELITES and that Jesus asks his disciples come down to this for us: "How shall I respond to the Lord?"

The God Who Questions

God directs more than 350 questions to us throughout Scripture. Some are repetitions, but in different contexts. There are even more questions that human beings address to God and to Jesus. Job, Jeremiah, and the psalmists anticipate many of our own questions, such as that burning one: "Why do the innocent suffer?" Very often we ask: "Does God, can God, really care about me personally?"

Many of the disciples' questions were a search for truth, but all too many were like these: "Who is greatest in the kingdom of heaven?" "How many times do I have to forgive?" "What reward will we get?" Other contemporaries of Jesus asked such questions as this: "What sign will you show us?"

God doesn't ask or respect questions of that caliber. Job had a lot of reasons to ask questions. He had been God's friend, and for no reason that Job could grasp, he seemingly lost that friendship and everything else besides, except his trust in God, trusting that God could be trusted. His three so-called friends argued with a great deal of traditional pious talk, insisting that obviously Job had sinned, for God would not let the innocent suffer. God, silent through a lot of this talk and through Job's anguished questions, finally said to Job what sounds like a reprimand: "Gird up your loins like a man; I will question you, and you declare to me" (Job 40:7). The Lord piled question upon question that led Job to see, in the power and majesty they revealed, that he was simply immersed in mystery, not merely in problems to which there could be an answer (Job 42:3).

We human questioners of God all too often get caught up in one of two errors:

- We may try to reduce mystery to problem. True mystery is a reality that is simply too deep for us to master. It is to be embraced and loved and searched ever deeper without ever exhausting it. Job said finally and simply, "See, I am of small account; what shall I answer you? I lay my hand on my mouth" (Job 40:4).

- Or we may make a game of questioning once we start, and then end up in confrontation rather than communication, seeking dominance rather than understanding or wisdom. Like the Pharisees questioning Jesus, we muffle the Spirit within us.

God's Questions

God's questions to human beings are different from many of ours. They are invitations to open our hearts and minds in a divine-human communication and relationship; *there* is mystery. The divine questioning respects human dignity and human freedom. God's questions are caring, even when they constitute a reprimand or a challenge, and they are not merely rhetorical. As from a good teacher, the question is put in order to open up new dimensions of understanding or elicit new insights, correct faulty views or establish new links between things already known. God's questions are personal, directed *to someone* or to a specific group.

We speak of seeking God, as we must, but there is an awesome mystery in God's seeking us. God does not force, but invites. Even better, God

*L*ate June 1940: I am preparing for reception into Saint Benedict's Convent [now Monastery]. The Benedictine monk retreat master begins with the words from Hosea, "I will allure her, I will lead her into the desert, and I will speak to her heart." Now, more than fifty years later, I know it was God's calling me by name, and a vocation within a vocation. It was a life-giving word initiating a long and hidden gestation.

—*Grace Notes*

attracts, appeals, as in Hosea: "I will now allure her [Israel], and bring her into the wilderness, and speak tenderly to her" (2:14). If we hear God's questions in the depth of our hearts, hearing personally as they are personally addressed, they will call us; they will challenge us; they will sometimes unsettle us. But they can bring us, by God's grace in the power of those words themselves and in us, to freedom, to more life, to deeper love.

Some refrains are helpful as reminders: Psalm 95:7-8, "O that today you would listen to his voice! Do not harden your hearts"; Jesus to the thief on the cross, "Today you will be with me in Paradise" (Luke 23:43); "This is the day that the LORD has made" (Psalm 118:24)—which applies to every day; "Morning by morning he wakens—wakens my ear to listen as those who are taught. The Lord GOD has opened my ear, and I was not rebellious, I did not turn backward" (Isaiah 50:4-5).

Where Are You?

God's first question is put to Adam and Eve after they eat the fruit that is both forbidden and enticing—beautiful to see, good to eat, and the tempter promises it will make them more like God. As we all know from experience, this is the prototype of all temptation. After they give in to the enticement, God asks Adam—and asks each of us—"Where are you?" (Genesis 3:9).

God, with them even in their sin, is revealed as relational with Adam— a relationship that was familiar and at peace before sin. Now God is severe but lovingly concerned. God is with them but they are not with God.

Being made in God's image is really our primal vocation. The deep call within us to be, and to become ever more, like the one in whose image we are made—this is also the ground for divine-human communication and communion, and the basis for the covenant bond. The book of Sirach has a beautiful, meditative description of God's loving gifts to Adam and Eve:

> The Lord created human beings out of earth. . . .
> He endowed them with strength like his own,
>   and made them in his own image. . . .

Discretion and tongue and eyes,
    ears and a mind for thinking he gave them.
He filled them with knowledge and understanding,
    and showed them good and evil.
He put the fear of him into their hearts
    to show them the majesty of his works. . . .
He bestowed knowledge upon them,
    and allotted to them the law of life.
He established with them an eternal covenant. (Sirach 17:1-12)

God spoke, but Adam and Eve hid. Are there times when God wished to reveal something in word or sacrament that would have given me deeper experience and/or knowledge of God and my relation to God or some direction for my life, and I went into hiding to escape the consequences? Might some event in my life have made clear a new responsibility while I, like Adam and Eve, hid? But we cannot hide from God: "'Who can hide in secret places so that I cannot see them?' says the LORD. 'Do I not fill heaven and earth?'" (Jeremiah 23:24).

When Adam and Eve hide from God, God comes to them and initiates communication with the simple question, "Where are you?" But Adam evades a direct answer, hardens his heart, and closes his mouth about their real situation. "I heard the sound of you in the garden, and I was afraid, because I was naked; and I hid myself" (Genesis 3:10). Notice that Adam doesn't say "we"—just "I" and "myself."

Call and Response

Later in Scripture God calls many who, unlike Adam, respond directly and immediately:

- Abraham, when told to sacrifice Isaac, responds immediately, "Here I am," and is willing to act, however painful the demand (Genesis 22:1).

- Moses, at the burning bush, says, "Here I am," though he is afraid of God's majesty (Exodus 3:4).

- Young Samuel, called in his sleep, is at first simply confused, but when he realizes it is the Lord, he announces without hesitation, "Speak, for your servant is listening" (1 Samuel 3:10).

- Isaiah responds to "Whom shall I send, and who will go for us?" with "Here am I; send me!" (Isaiah 6:8).

- After recapitulating the long list of those ready to answer God fully and freely, the Letter to the Hebrews (10:5-7) says of Christ that when he came into the world to fulfill the New Covenant, he said, "See, God, I have come to do your will."

But Adam avoids the question, saying not where he was but that he hid in fear because he was naked. He does not admit immediately and openly that he was disobedient, and that it was in consequence of this that he knew he was naked. In the deepest sense Adam refused to be naked before God—he turned from God and hid because of sin. Just before the story of the first sin we read: "And the man and his wife were both naked, and were not ashamed" (Genesis 2:25). Adam and Eve came naked and holy from the creative hand of God. Saint Jerome took as his motto, "Naked to follow the naked Christ." Saint Francis of Assisi literally stripped off his fine clothing as a sign, almost a kind of sacrament, of his utter poverty before Christ and his utter self-giving to Christ—the Christ who gave himself to us and for us, and who died naked on the Cross for Adam's and our salvation. Was it, then, Adam's nakedness that caused him to be so fearful? Or was it sin that made him see nakedness as fearful, that distorted his perception and his response?

Do we hide from the full truth about ourselves, our thoughts and actions, by evasion, self-justification, defensiveness—even by cultivating frenetic activity and preoccupation? By frequently seeking diversion so we don't have to face ourselves? By centering on ourselves and the wants that self keeps before us?

In the Genesis story, the complications of sin compound. When God asks outright about their disobedience, Adam blames Eve and Eve blames the serpent. Does this have an uncomfortable familiarity about it?

At the end of the story, just before Adam and Eve are sent out of Paradise, there is a quiet concluding verse: "And the LORD God made garments of skins for the man and for his wife, and clothed them" (Genesis 3:21). This brings out another dimension of the whole tragic sequence. God had wanted simply to give our first parents all the wonderful gifts of divine creative love. They, however, wanted power and mastery, and they violated their deepest selves as well as their relation with God to get it. The God they had hidden from sought them out in mercy and promised them redemption. This is a love story. It is the ultimate love story.

Very soon other questions related to "Where are you?" occur in Scripture. In the next chapter of Genesis (4:9), God asks Cain, "Where is your brother Abel?" God asks Hagar, when she is fleeing with her little son to the desert from Abraham and Sarah's house, "Where have you come from and where are you going?" (Genesis 16:8). Of Elijah God asks, "What are you doing here?" (1 Kings 19:9). Saint Bernard repeatedly asked his monks, "Why have you come here?"

These may well be questions that God asks of us: Where are your sister and your brother in Christ? What have you had to do with their being where they are? Where have you come in your life's experience to be where you are now spiritually? Where are you going from here? What are you doing here?

Chapter 11

What Are You Looking For?

OD ASKED ADAM, "WHERE ARE YOU?" Throughout history, God's people have asked back, "Where is our God?" and their neighbors have added their counterpoint: "Where *is* your God?" In Scripture God's answer is this: God is precisely where God has chosen to be—with us, with God's people.

Adam was in hiding, afraid of God and of his nakedness before God, avoiding God's probing question, trying to circumvent responsibility. Where are we now, before the Lord who made us, made us in the divine image, and graced us for a life of intimacy with God? When that question was asked of Adam, who had known God's presence with him in the garden, he knew that the Lord was present even now, even in his sin.

Sacred history is bound together with a lifeline of that loving, active presence of God. It is a history of expanding the boundaries of the divine relationship with God's people, of deepening intimacy, of the mystery of Uncreated Love poured out on created beings for fullness of life. It is the mystery of covenant that suffuses the Old and New Testaments. To individuals and to the community the promise is this: "I am with you—I will be with you! Do not fear!" Abraham, Moses, David, Isaiah, Jeremiah, Ezekiel—all of them communicated God's promise of presence. Ezekiel's

130

prophecy, ending with his vision of rebuilding Jerusalem and the Temple, concludes: "And the name of the city from that time on shall be, The LORD is There" (Ezekiel 48:35).

In the Old Testament, the people are assured of God's presence by means of signs—the burning bush, the ark of the covenant, and many others. In the New Testament God becomes one of us, not just a sign. God spoke through the prophets; Jesus was and is the very Word of God. A great temple had been built for the Lord; Jesus is the living temple, and makes living stones of us who have become temples of the Spirit. God gave the Law as loving direction for living the gift of life; Jesus is and gives the gospel, the Good News that fulfills the Law.

Any one of us could multiply the evidences of this mystery of profound transformation, attesting to deep, developing, overflowing life the life of God shared ever more completely with human beings. What a magnificent answer God has given and gives to any one who asks, "Where is our God?" "Where is your God?" God is with us. More than that, Paul speaks of "the glory of this mystery, which is Christ in you" (Colossians 1:27).

What Are You Looking For?

But again: What of God's questions to us? From the first question of the Lord in Genesis we go to the first question of Jesus in John's Gospel. It hinges on where we are and where we think God is. Andrew and Simon, who had been disciples of John the Baptist, turn to Jesus and follow him when John identifies him as the Lamb of God. Immediately Jesus asks them, "What are you looking for?" (John 1:38). Jesus asked his prospective disciples, and asks each of us today, "What are you really looking for?" The answer to this question has significant consequences, as Peter and Andrew and James and John and all who became Jesus' followers were to find out, sometimes to their pain and sorrow but ultimately to their great joy.

"What are you really looking for?" is a momentous question, because what or whom we desire is who we really are. A wonderful little fourteenth-century treatise on spirituality, *The Cloud of Unknowing*, concludes "It is not what you are nor what you have been that God sees with his all-merciful eyes, but what you desire to be." In the three years of intensive formation of his disciples, Jesus left them in no doubt about what he was looking for. Time after time he led them by word and by living example to face the choices involved, the commitment and fidelity required of him and of them. It was an arduous schooling, and though they loved the Master, they often failed to understand him or to measure up to what he was looking for. Perhaps when they came to him initially they were simultaneously attracted and scared, sensing they would have to let themselves be transformed.

Jesus had to lead and heal them from desires unworthy of who they were as human beings, as images of God, as disciples, and eventually as apostles able to carry forward his message and his mission. He had to teach them and ultimately grace them into desires worthy of who they were and *whom they were called to be.* Sometimes they hardly had even basic necessities, yet when Jesus asked them if they had lacked anything when he sent them out on mission with so little, they answered immediately and simply: "No, not a thing" (Luke 22:35).

We live in a madly consumerist age, culture, and society. At the same time there is grinding poverty, an increasing chasm between the rich and poor. There are hungry children, hopeless adults, the homeless, aged who are fearful and who have lost hope, the sick, people who are not adequately—and surely not lovingly—cared for. God asked Cain, "Where is your brother?" We are Jesus' disciples; what would he say to us, to you, to me, personally, today?

True Authority

Jesus drew a young child to himself and called on the disciples to become as the child, and thus become the greatest in the kingdom (Matthew 18). A child has no worldly power or worldly influence—often a lot of influence but not worldly influence—is wholly dependent, with no one under his or her authority, no perks to give in order to secure power or influence. It is only what Jesus asked of himself. He emptied himself, not clinging to all that belonged to him as God, all that he could have rightfully claimed. He chose, rather, to become human, a unique self-emptying, a mystery of total self-giving. He humbled himself even to the point of the most despicable kind of death known to his time. He emptied himself, humbled himself, and then God raised him up, exalted him (Philippians 2:6-11).

Cardinal Bernardin of Chicago accepted being stripped down to his fundamental humanity and his sonship in Christ. Criticized by people and by his priests for what they called the "plush" surroundings in which the archbishop lived, he had a deep inner conversion and interior re-fashioning of his life. Falsely charged with sexual misconduct, he reconciled with the recanting accuser. Finally, his experience with pancreatic cancer turned his pastoral work to the seriously ill. What an immense influence Bernardin had in his last years—not just influence with those who shared his faith, but with many who did not. He emptied himself and God helped him empty himself. And then the depth and quality, the real influence was manifest. I think of Mother Teresa and receiving from her a series of transparently simple, transparently self-emptying letters that the world would treasure today.

We live in an age, a culture, and society that is often ruthlessly competitive in precisely those things that tempted the disciples of Jesus—power, position, success by the world's standards. Can we really say we embrace the gospel ideal, Jesus' chosen values? He had no significant worldly position. It is true that he was addressed as Master and Rabbi by many, but his was a leadership of attraction and challenge rather than control or dominance. Undoubtedly Christ had immense power to heal all kinds of blindness and deafness and lameness, power to give hope and comfort, to attract many people—but he never sought power and he used it expressly for others. When, because of his great deeds, the people wanted to make him king, he simply disappeared.

It is striking that the people spoke of his innate authority more frequently than of his power. They were astounded at his teaching, saying that he taught as one having authority, not as the Scribes who had position and power. Jesus had authority—an inner authority from a depth and wholeness within the person. That inner authority, that authenticity, gives weight to one's words in a way the person doesn't seek or manipulate. It is simply an overflow of who the person is. And Jesus knew who he was.

I came to the orphanage to teach, in love with knowledge, a little drunk on what I had acquired, hungry for more, and pretty much a "heady" person. I made the stupid mistakes of the inexperienced, not recognizing how far my language and my procedure were from the students' experience. But then the slow and long-unrecognized transformation began—one that was to deeply affect all my teaching years. I began to hear those children's stories, often awful stories. My heart went into gear and my head functioned in its service. As I got to know them I realized they had, and would likely always have, need of all they could learn, and that they would probably learn what they loved. They taught me to be a teacher, by re-routing my head trips into and through my heart.

—*Grace Notes*

Discovery of Our True Self

In the first chapter of John's Gospel, Jesus asks those who are to become his apostles, "What are you looking for?" Near the end of the gospel, when Jesus meets Mary Magdalene at the tomb, he asks her: "Whom are you looking for?" (John 20:15). No longer *what* are you looking for but *whom*. When he then addresses her by name, she recognizes him and is sent rejoicing to tell the others that she has found him abundantly alive.

The foundation of our longing, our searching, for God is this: deep in our very being we are each made in God's image, a bond that endlessly attracts us beyond ourselves. It is a kind of homing instinct, a hungering and thirsting for God of which the Psalms and Isaiah speak so frequently and so vividly. The very language of hunger and thirst suggests the need to sustain life—the hunger and thirst of the heart, of the spirit.

Perhaps if Jesus were teaching his disciples in today's world, he would adopt something like the contrast of true and false self that Thomas Merton made so widely known. Though we may think of it as something quite contemporary, it is directly from Scripture: "You were taught to put away your former way of life, your old self, . . . and to be renewed in the spirit of your minds, and to clothe yourselves with the new self, created according to the likeness of God in true righteousness and holiness" (Ephesians 4:22-24). Serving the false self cannot bring fulfillment to the true self. The Beatitudes turn the world of the false self upside down. Jesus calls his disciples to self-transcendence for the sake of fullness of life and for an abundant overflow into the life of others.

In the Synoptic Gospels (Matthew 10; Mark 8; Luke 9) Jesus says in slightly varying ways that the person who seeks his or her own life—the limited, narrow life of the false self—will lose that very life, but anyone who loses—that is, transcends or goes beyond that limited life of the false self for Jesus' sake and the sake of the gospel—will find true life. The *New English Bible* translation makes the point crystal clear: "What does a man gain by winning the whole world at the cost of his true self? What can he give to buy that self back?" (Mark 8:36-37).

Thomas Merton is eloquent on this subject. "Unless we discover this deep self, which is hidden with Christ in God, we will never really know ourselves as persons. . . . And indeed, if we seek our true selves it is not in order to contemplate ourselves, but to pass beyond ourselves and find God." This losing the self in the gospel sense is not alienation of that self, but the most perfect self-realization. Nor does the search for the true self isolate us from others. "A person cannot enter into the deepest center of himself and pass through that center into God unless he is able to pass entirely out of himself, empty himself and give himself to others in the purity of selfless love." And so this becomes a whole life, a deeper and more true life within, a deepened relationship with God, a more free and full relation with others.

There is so deep a mystery of the divine life in us that for a long time it may all sound very unreal, or wholly beyond our comprehension, even when we are adults. When we are young and ambitious, responding to a culture that demands that we prove ourselves, compete and achieve, we may not be very attracted to or concerned about this life in mystery. It may be that only when life experience and grace combine to open our minds and hearts that we see how empty life would be if getting ahead were all there is. Then our deeper hungers can assert themselves, and if we attend to them, this self-transcending life becomes increasingly desirable.

To go back a long way, Jan van Ruysbroeck described it this way in the fourteenth century: "When we transcend ourselves [that is, our narrow, self-regarding selves] and become in our ascent towards God so simple that the bare supreme love can lay hold of us, then we cease, and we and all our selfhood die in God. And in this death we become the hidden children of God, and find a new life within us." This truly is the mystical life, the life we were made for, the life we are called to in the depths of our being, made in the divine image and baptized into divine life.

So, when Jesus asks, "What are you seeking?" and ultimately "Whom are you seeking?" we might well answer "God" or "my true self," for there I am the dwelling of the three-personed God. This is to live a holy life, as we are called by God and graced by God to live. And God will bring that call and grace to fruition if we truly seek. Jeremiah speaks for God when he assures Israel and us: "When you search for me, you will find me; if you seek me with all your heart" (Jeremiah 29:13).

The Second Vatican Council devoted an entire chapter of its principal document, Dogmatic Constitution on the Church (*Lumen Gentium*), to the universal call to holiness—every person is called to live a holy life. "Holy" is sometimes used as if holiness cuts one off from other people. The reverse is true: holiness is our fundamental vocation, and it binds us most deeply to others—to all others. One is reminded of the final sentence of Leon Bloy's book, *The Woman Who Was Poor*: "There is only one misery—not to be a saint."

The life of seeking is a life, and a lifetime's vocation. It is meant as a time to grow, to deepen, to be purified, to overflow to others and for others. *The Cloud of Unknowing*, referred to earlier, says this: "If you wish to keep growing you must nourish in your heart the lively longing for God. Though this loving desire is certainly God's gift, it is up to you to nurture it." And this is beautifully illustrated in the familiar story from the Desert Fathers that I cited near the beginning of this book—when Abba Lot listed his spiritual disciplines to his spiritual father Abba Joseph and then asked "What else can I do?" Abba Joseph stood up, stretched his hands toward heaven, his fingers like ten lamps of fire, and said, "If you will, you can become all flame."

Chapter 12

Who Do You Say That I Am?

ESUS OFTEN WENT TO THE HILLS or the desert to pray—sometimes alone, other times with a few disciples. On one occasion he asked them, "Who do people say that I am?" Then: "Who do *you* say that I am?" (Matthew 16:13-15; Mark 8:27-29; Luke 9:18-20). And immediately after, Jesus foretells his suffering and death, and warns the disciples of the cost of discipleship—losing, transcending their false selves. Then comes the Transfiguration. The whole event is a watershed in the life of Christ and of his disciples.

"Who do people say that I am?" It is from others that we learn our faith; currents of opinion and expression can affect our faith deeply. As I noted earlier, some years ago it was common to call Jesus "the man for others." He surely was the man for others, but he was the man for others because he was the man for his Father who sent him to the others. If we get caught up in current phrasing, we can lose sight of the depth and range of faith's mystery.

"Who do others say that I am?" can be a halting point if we merely repeat what others say or, with all good will, recite a formula of faith. This is particularly seductive for students and scholars of the Bible, for whom having to know which biblical scholar said what about Jesus can be a trap.

In the gospels, the disciples answer that people are saying Jesus is John the Baptist come back to life, or Elijah, or one of the prophets. "Prophet" was the greatest call and role they knew. There had been none recognized for hundreds of years, and the people longed for the promised prophet like Moses.

What others were saying—even their recognition of him as prophet— had value; but Jesus asked the disciples—and he asks us—to go beyond this level of knowing. He asked and he asks the very personal question, the one that matters ultimately: "Who do you say that I am?"

Each evangelist notes that Simon answered, "the Messiah." Luke adds, "the Messiah of God," and Matthew, "the Messiah, the Son of the Living God"—all of them affirming that he is more than a prophet. Matthew has Jesus say to Simon, "Blessed are you," assuring him that this recognition is not a human insight but a gift of God. Jesus then gives him the new name, Peter the Rock. Our thoughts may go immediately to Peter's inconstancy in the rest of the gospel—impassioned avowals of love and fidelity that disintegrate under pressure and threat. This man, the Rock? But then we think also of the Peter who wept and the Peter of the Acts of the Apostles who has been transformed by the gift of the Spirit. Our weakness finds strength both in Jesus' trusting so mercurial a man and in the belief that the same Spirit is given to us.

Our Response to Our Questioning God

As Christ asks us—asks you, asks me—who we say he is, we are surely on solid ground in responding with Peter and the creedal professions, "Messiah, Son of the living God." But we are not asked the question at one definitive time (except maybe at our death) or only once. I am asked again and again, in times of joy and of pain, sometimes of anguish, as I experience life, grow up, grow old. We might well answer the Lord differently at different times.

In all this variety of experience, Hosea (6:3) would urge us as he urged his own generation: "Let us press on to know the LORD." In Scripture, "to know" does not mean only or essentially intellectual knowledge, but heart knowledge, intimacy. And Hosea continues in the same verse: "He will come to us like the showers, like the spring rains that water the earth." The Lord invites us, allures us, seeks to be known by us.

What if Jesus stood before you now and asked you, as a profoundly personal question, "Who do *you* say that I am?" Maybe your response would be beyond Peter's answer and the church's formulations. Maybe your own experiences have helped you, by the grace of God, to press on to know the Lord in very personal ways.

Maybe insights and events in your life, enlightened by Scripture, have helped you to see Jesus as the Way: the way to the Father, the way to live now, trying to live by Jesus' commandment of love and the life of his Spirit within you and eternal life as the fruit of the way. Saint Thomas Aquinas, commenting on John 14:6, says that Jesus "is himself at once both the way and the goal. In his human nature he is the way, and in his divine nature he is the goal. . . . Christ is the way by which we come to know truth, though he is also that truth." And then he adds: "It is better to limp along the way than to stride along off the way." I may limp along the true way and seem to advance but little, yet I move toward the goal. Tireless running on the wrong road only takes me ever farther from the goal, "Christ the Way"— the Christ who said, "I am the Way." And to be on the way is itself a kind of arrival; to seek Jesus as the Way is already to have been found by him.

Or maybe Jesus as Truth is how you know him best: Christ as God's full self-revelation to us, Jesus the courageous truth-teller, the "Yes!" to the Father. The truth who will make us, and make you, free.

Perhaps you are most attracted to Jesus as Life. Jesus' story and his parables are so full of life—created life, true life, life with God, life in God, eternal life—abundant life as the purpose of his coming and of his paschal mystery; Jesus healing lives, restoring lives, serving the life-needs of the poor, the rejected, those in need of forgiveness, and you yourself in any of these conditions.

It may be that Light, Jesus as Light of the World, your light in the world, best speaks your attraction to Christ. Light makes seeing possible, gives life and color to the world, transforms darkness. "In your light we see light" (Psalm 36:9). And see our way—see truly.

Or maybe you press on to know the Lord most deeply as Love—love incarnate, the one you love or seek to love with all your being, the one whose love is your greatest treasure. This gift may well draw out your deepest longing, your deepest gratitude, and your deepest desire to serve.

Jesus has proclaimed that he is all these and more. I need all these ways of saying who he is, and who he can be for me now. But each of us, at particular times in our lives, will likely have a specific attraction, a very personal way of identifying Christ that touches us most deeply then. And by the grace of God, when we embrace any of them, others will open to us.

Reconciliation of Apparent Opposites

If I were asked which has been the most profound for me, I would say that increasingly it has been Jesus, Lord of Life, and Jesus, Incarnate Love. But another has come into focus and become a gift in pressing on to know the Lord. It is Christ's reconciliation of apparent opposites, his embracing all that is real, choosing such radically contrasting people as disciples, and progressively drawing them into real community. I suspect that awareness of the world's needs, the church's needs, monastic needs, and this octogenarian's reflective look at her own life make this reconciliation of opposites so important to me now.

Primary among these seeming contraries is divine and human. It is not a problem to be solved but a mystery that invites an ever-deeper living-with, living-in. Stretching the mind is simply not enough; as Job says finally, "I lay my hand on my mouth" (Job 40:4). I must allow God to open my heart to rest in the reality that Jesus became one of us, and that in his depths and for our sake he embodies the dialogue of love between God and human beings.

Another of the seeming contraries that Jesus brings to wholeness is the incarnational and the eschatological, or, in simpler language, this world and the world to come, the "already" and the "not yet." In the life of the church we never seem able to keep them in living tension. Jesus deeply respected the created world. He was actively involved in caring for the genuine earthly needs of people, even strangers and outcasts, and he was outspoken about problems and issues in his time, yet he always called people beyond the present to the fullness of the Kingdom in forming their values and judging their actions.

Another seeming contrary, seen by many as a contradiction: unity and diversity. We may distort the idea of unity to a uniformity that is destructive of true unity. Then the temptation is to champion diversity. Jesus opposed the rigid and unnecessary uniformities demanded by the Pharisees, while preaching a love that was the very ground of unity. He accepted a great diversity of personalities even among his apostles, but sought to bring them into a loving, serving community. Then as the fruit of the paschal mystery he gave us the prototype for relating unity and diversity: the Body of Christ—in Paul's words (1 Corinthians 12), the diversity of gifts and the diversity of members in the one Body—diversity serving a richer unity and unity embracing diversity.

A final example of seeming contraries: the old and the new. Jesus was devoted to much of the old, but to the heart of it, the living center of the old. As he said to his accusers, he did not come to destroy the Law but to fulfill it—and in fulfilling it he brought newness. Isaiah (43:19) alerts his hearers to coming change when the Lord says, "I am about to do a new thing; . . . do you not perceive it?" and a little later (48:6), "From this time forward I make you hear new things, hidden things that you have not known." Throughout the prophets there are promises of newness—newness that Christ brings to realization in the New Covenant, the New Law, the New Creation, the new heart, the new name, the New Jerusalem, and the expectation of new heavens and a new earth. Jesus had the fidelity to be true to what was central and perduring in the Old Covenant, and he had the courage to proclaim the New. Jesus saw that the Holy Spirit would make known to us many things he himself did not reveal (John 14). In being profoundly, radically true to the heart of the old, Jesus was radically new.

We return to Jesus' question as addressed to each of us and to the whole community of faith: "Who do you say that I am?" We must and we do say with Peter, "You are the Messiah, the Son of the living God." But we have so much of Scripture, such a long living tradition in Christian devotion, and our own unique experience to open that treasure chest of a response. With the eyes and ears and hearts of faith, we may make this profession of faith deeply personal, deeply prayerful, and deeply transforming.

Chapter 13

Will You Turn Back and Live?

"THE KINGDOM OF GOD HAS COME NEAR; repent, and believe in the good news." According to Mark (1:15), these words open Jesus' ministry. Throughout Scripture, genuine repentance and genuine faith are required of God's people.

Our Need for Repentance and Reconciliation

Jeremiah (8:4) speaks for the Lord when he asks, "When people fall, do they not get up again? If they go astray, do they not turn back?" Similarly, Ezekiel (18:23): "Have I any pleasure in the death of the wicked, says the Lord GOD, and not rather that they should turn from their ways and live?" The connection between repentance and life, truly living, is very nearly a refrain.

Paul speaks for all of us: "I do not understand my own actions. For I do not do what I want, but I do the very thing I hate. . . . For I do not do the good I want, but the evil I do not want is what I do. . . . When I want to do what is good, evil lies close at hand" (Romans 7:15-21). With the psalmist we take comfort in the assurance that God "knows how we were made; he remembers that we are dust" (Psalm 103:14). Of course we are not *only* dust—we are God's creation, in God's own likeness, destined for fullness of life with God. While we are weakened by the sinful condition into which we were born and by the effects of our own sins, we are strengthened, healed, and restored by the grace of God if we cooperate with that gift.

God made us for life. Throughout Scripture sin is associated with death, and it is a dying. Again and again God calls to the sinful person, the sinful community, as he does in Ezekiel (33:11): "Turn back, turn back from your evil ways; for why will you die?" Adam and Eve were told that eating the forbidden fruit would cause their death. They died to innocence, to familiarity with God, to unity within themselves and between themselves, to harmony with the rest of creation.

In Luke's account of the Prodigal Son, the father—who was truly prodigal with his love and forgiveness—speaks of his wayward son to the elder brother who lacked a forgiving heart: "This brother of yours was dead and has come to life" (Luke 15:32). The younger son "came to himself" (15:17) and returned to his father. There is no impassioned plea for forgiveness; he says only "Father!" (15:18).

Awareness of God's Desire to Forgive

Our need for reconciliation begins with temptation, which we tend to think of only negatively and with pain. But remembering the temptation of Jesus right after his baptism and before he began his public ministry gives a different perspective. The Spirit who descended on Jesus at baptism led, even "drove" (Mark 1:12) him into the wilderness to be tempted. If Jesus was tempted as a human being, how should we escape it? If he had to decide how he was going to live the life and mission given him by his Father—if the Master had to do that, then surely the disciples.

Will the decision be for God's way or Satan's way? Was this an anticipation of Jesus' calling Peter "Satan" (Matthew 16:23) when Peter tried to dissuade Jesus from accepting the Passion? Did the dismissal of Peter's proposal remind Jesus of his dismissal of Satan in the desert? If Jesus was led or driven by the Spirit—and the gospel says that Jesus was led

$\mathcal{Y}$ou, God, have allured me; sometimes, like my patron [the prophet Jeremiah = Jeremy], I have felt that you duped me. You have given me no escape and no reprieve from yearning, longing. You have led me into desert places again and again—the place of your own temptation and the places of mine, the place of your mysterious purifying care of my spirit even in failure, the places of my driving thirst and my sometimes frantic searching for "a way" in what seemed like trackless immensity.

—*Grace Notes*

there purposely to be tempted—then the ultimate meaning is for *life*, not death. Can we see the temptations in our lives as meant for life?

We know how Jesus dealt with temptation. He called on the word of God his Father, familiar words from Deuteronomy and the Psalms, words that came spontaneously. He responded as a Son so that we might learn to respond as disciples invited into filial relation to God, our Father.

We know all too well that we do not always come out of temptation unscathed as Jesus did. We do sin and sin is real in our lives. But just as truly as we should not minimize it, neither should we be preoccupied with it. It is not the primary focus; the gospel is the Good News, not the bad news. Paul makes a very strong point of this when he speaks of a whole sequence of situations associated with sin (Romans 5), and rings the changes on this refrain: "grace abounded all the more." *Much more* God's gift! *Much* more! There, in the light of the gospel, is where the focus ought to be. Still, we do need to be direct and honest about our sins and our sinfulness—with ourselves, before God, and in matters of confession in the sacrament of reconciliation.

But while I need to judge my own sins realistically, other peoples' faults and sins are not mine to judge, however much I might like to. "Why do you see the speck in your neighbor's eye, but do not notice the log in your own eye?" (Matthew 7:3). "Do not judge, and you will not be judged" (Luke 6:37). The Desert Fathers, as usual, are instructive. Recall the story, recounted earlier, of Abba Moses, former robber, who carried a leaky jug and said, "My sins run out behind me and I do not see them. And today I am coming to judge the errors of another."

When we do sin, we are called to genuine repentance. Scripture is full of the terms, "turn, return, repent." Repentance involves genuine sorrow, with the primary focus on God. When I was younger—perhaps there are remnants of it still—I tended to become remorseful rather than truly repentant. Remorse may simply be distress or even anguish that I have done this, with the focus on myself, on my failure, and it may reveal a good deal of pride or vanity. Remorse leaves me with the burden of guilt. Repentance calls for and secures God's mercy and healing.

There are rich nuances in the scriptural calls to repentance. "Return to me, says the LORD of hosts, and I will return to you" (Zechariah 1:3). "The

Israelites shall return and seek the LORD their God . . . ; they shall come in awe to the LORD and to his goodness" (Hosea 3:5). "The LORD your God is gracious and merciful, and will not always turn away his face from you, if you return to him" (2 Chronicles 30:9). Ezekiel (30:31) exhorts the people: "Repent and turn from all your transgressions; . . . and get yourselves a new heart and a new spirit." Hosea (6:1-2) combines the call with the promise—"Come, let us return to the LORD; . . . he has struck down, and he will bind us up. After two days he will revive us; on the third day we will raise us up, that we may live before him"—live in greater and greater fullness of life after the death of sin.

Repentance surfaces repeatedly in the New Testament as well. It had been the central message of John the Baptist, and Jesus, who had nothing to repent of, joined humanity in that baptism of repentance, again emptying himself, humbling himself for our sake. The first words of Jesus in Mark's Gospel are an echo of John: "Repent, and believe in the good news"—turn away from; turn to. This fundamental message pervades the gospels—Jesus came to call not the righteous but sinners (Matthew 9:13; Mark 2:17; Luke 5:32). Paul adds another note, describing the content of his preaching to Jews and Gentiles—"repent, and turn to God, and do deeds consistent with repentance" (Acts 26:20). So repentance involves both a disposition of the heart and commensurate action.

God's Merciful Love

God's mercy embraces our repentance. "The steadfast love of the LORD never ceases, his mercies never come to an end; they are new every morning; great is your faithfulness." These words from Lamentations (3:22-23) do not sound at all like a lament. They are a prayer of confidence, of loving acceptance of God's compassion, his mercy. The prayer in Wisdom (11:23–12:2) surely instructs our hearts:

> You are merciful to all, for you can do all things,
> and you overlook people's sins, so that they may repent.
> For you love all things that exist,
> and detest none of the things that you have made. . . .
> You spare all things, for they are yours, O Lord, you who love the living.

For your immortal spirit is in all things.
Therefore you correct little by little those who trespass,
and you remind and warn them of the things through which they sin,
so that they may be freed from wickedness and put their trust in you, O Lord.

The familiar words of Joel (2:12-13) are incorporated into many communal penance services: "Return to me with all your heart. . . . Return to the LORD, your God, for he is gracious and merciful, slow to anger, and abounding in steadfast love." And the gospels are rich in accounts of Christ's mercy to sinners. "Has no one condemned you? . . . Neither do I condemn you. Go your way, and from now on do not sin again" (John 8:10-11).

The early monks who knew their sinfulness also knew God's mercy and were brought to being merciful themselves. "An elder was asked by a certain soldier if God would forgive a sinner. And he said to him: Tell me, beloved, if your cloak is torn, will you throw it away? The soldier replied and said: No. I will mend it and put it back on. The elder said to him: If you take care of your cloak, will God not be merciful to his own image?" Many people think of those Desert Fathers and Mothers as a species of strange, crusty old men and a few women—at least we know of only a few—who were living a difficult life and making life difficult for everybody else. But they are among the most compassionate people we will ever meet. With a profound sense of their own weakness, they have a heart of mercy for every one else who is weak.

God's mercy brings repentant sinners forgiveness, restoration, and healing. "To those who repent he grants a return, and he encourages those who are losing hope. . . . How great is the mercy of the Lord, and his forgiveness for those who return to him!" (Sirach 17:24, 29). When Ezekiel (18:31) tells Israel—and us—to get "a new heart and a new spirit," he makes it clear that what we cannot get for ourselves, God wills to give us, and we can receive it. "I will take the people of Israel from the nations among which they have gone, and will gather them from every quarter, and bring them to their own land" (Ezekiel 37:21). We all stray into territory that is alien to our true selves and to our professed fidelity to God. "I will sprinkle clean water upon you, and you shall be clean from all your uncleannesses, and from all your idols I will cleanse you" (Ezekiel 36:25). Idols may well appear in our response to the question, "What are you looking for?" Yet even when we get it all wrong, God's promise stands: "I will give them one heart, and put a new spirit within them; I will remove the heart of stone from their flesh and give them a heart of flesh. . . . Then they shall be my people, and I will be their God" (Ezekiel 11:19-20).

In the New Covenant Jesus heals diseased and deformed bodies, and since the body and spirit are so intertwined, he also forgives sins, restoring total health. The healing of the body is a kind of sacrament of the healing of the spirit. And his final word is so often, "Go in peace!"

Abbot John Eudes Bamberger was a monk of Gethsemani Abbey and knew Thomas Merton well. He tells of Merton's life-long consciousness of being a forgiven sinner, with a story parallel to Saint Augustine's—a very long conversion process, not only from his sins but from his culture and his society, so that his mind and heart were turned in another direction and he was ready to accept the Lord. Augustine summed up his own life with startling clarity in a phrase we noted earlier in discussing reconciliation and healing as a fruit of monastic life: "What calls for all our efforts in this life is the healing of the eyes of our hearts, with which God is to be seen." Both Augustine and Merton wrote confessions, and neither is only or even primarily a confession of sin. Much more are they confessions of praise and thanksgiving for God's mercy.

Stories of forgiveness and healing assure me of mercy available to me, so I like them. But the real test is whether I am willing to be a forgiver and healer—wounded, to be sure, but willing, wanting to be merciful. We all have our own unique collection of weaknesses and sins. Sometimes we may be like Abba Ammonas in the desert who said, "I have spent fourteen years in [the desert] asking God night and day to grant me the victory over anger." We may be discouraged because we seem to have the same sins to confess over and over. Psalm 3 says the Lord remembers that we are dust. Our part is to recognize our weaknesses and failures and our need of healing, to believe that the steadfastly loving God holds out mercy and healing to us, to strive to respond to that love with an ever-deeper love of our own that will progressively "heal the eye of the heart by which we see God."

Forgiving Ourselves

C. S. Lewis reminds us of another dimension of repentance and forgiveness: "I think that if God forgives us, we must forgive ourselves.

Otherwise it is almost like setting ourselves up as a higher tribunal than God's." With King Hezekiah I can pray in peace and gratitude, "You have cast all my sins behind your back." And I can join him in blessing God as he prays, "The living, the living, they thank you, as I do this day" (Isaiah 38:17, 19). We live anew in God's forgiveness, his loving mercy.

Having received mercy and been graced with forgiveness, we should be joyful, but we may not always experience that joy. Is it perhaps because we are then looking at ourselves instead of looking at God and the gift of God? Maybe joy is one of the things we learn as our lives go on, our self-sufficiency proves painfully inadequate, our need of God and our desire deepens, and God's grace opens our hearts to know his re-creative love.

The word joy, *gaudium*, occurs only twice in the Rule, both times in the chapter on Lent. We are "to wash away in this holy season the negligences of other times" by such means as "compunction of heart and self-denial" so that we have something "to offer God of his own will *with the joy of the Holy Spirit* (1 Thess 1:6)" (49:3, 4, 6). Thus, says Benedict, we are to "look forward to holy Easter with joy and spiritual longing" (49:7).

Chapter 14

Where Is Your Faith?

"HE KINGDOM OF GOD HAS COME NEAR; repent and believe in the good news" (Mark 1:15). We have heard God's call to repentance. What is "believing the good news"?

One day, after a period of intense preaching in company with his closest followers, Jesus got into a boat to go across the lake. He fell asleep. A strong windstorm blew up, and when the disciples realized their boat was being swamped, they woke Jesus: "Teacher, do you not care that we are perishing?" He rebuked the wind and the waves, and then said to the disciples, "Why are you afraid? Have you still no faith?" (Mark 4:37-40).

Faith, a Gift from God

They said to one another, "Who then is this, that even the wind and the sea obey him?" (Mark 4:41). This took place a little while before Jesus asked them point blank, "Who do you say that I am?" But notice that they are saying, "Who is this?" They went to him for help though *they* were the sailors. His response implies, "Didn't you know that if I am with you, you are safe?" The gospel says they were amazed and afraid—Jesus and his actions were beyond their comprehension.

"Who is he?" They keep asking this through all their time with him, even after their profession of faith at the Transfiguration—and all the while Jesus is trying to build and elicit real faith. The scriptural understanding of faith is different from our common understanding of a profession of faith or "keeping the faith." Of course I am not belittling the church's formal professions of faith, the creeds, which articulate and preserve the essential tenets of gospel faith for current and succeeding generations. Nor do I wish to disparage any sincere use of the familiar phrase, "Keep the faith." But we must do more than simply accept a set of beliefs. The biblical understanding is deeply personal, relational, a trust in and commitment to Christ, to God.

In Christian faith, it is ultimately God who is believed, and that very faith is a gift of God, a grace. We can and must nourish and deepen it, but we cannot claim it or achieve it on our own. Its fulfillment is love: "I pray . . . that Christ may dwell in your hearts through faith, as you are being rooted and grounded in love" (Ephesians 3:17). And to the Galatians (5:6), drawing a contrast between living by faith and living by the law as he had once done, Paul writes: "The only thing that counts is faith working through love."

As surely as faith is a gift, one I certainly cannot take for granted, it is a necessity for life, for real life. Isaiah (7:9) says bluntly, "If you do not stand firm in faith, you shall not stand at all." Throughout the Bible, and especially in the Psalms, there are frequent references to the faithfulness of God, God's constancy in love, as ground for the believer's faith. Chapter 11 of the Letter to the Hebrews, which defines faith as "the assurance of things hoped for, the conviction of things not seen," provides a family history of some of the outstanding believers among our Old Testament forebears in faith, calling them "so great a cloud of witnesses" who encourage us down through the ages to live by faith as they did.

The conviction of things not seen is echoed by Paul in 2 Corinthians (5:7): "We walk by faith, not by sight." We know by experience that to "walk by faith and not by sight" can be a challenge. Often when Matthew tells of Jesus curing the blind, he talks also about the disciples' struggles with faith—a kind of blindness on their part—and Jesus takes the limitations of the physically blind as a symbol of the blindness that the disciples

are experiencing. Jesus cured both types of blindness, the physical usually more quickly. Jesus frequently chides and challenges the disciples for
this blindness, this lack of live and vibrant faith. Again and again he asks,
"Do you believe this?" "Do you believe that I am able to do this?" "Do you
believe in the Son of Man?" "Do you not believe that I am in the Father
and the Father is in me?" "Have I been with you all this time and you still
do not really know me?" "Do you really believe?" And again, *"Now* do you
believe?"

These questions reverberate through John's Gospel, but John uses the
active verb "to believe" much more frequently than the noun, "faith." In
fact, the verb occurs ninety-eight times in John as against thirty-five times
in the other three gospels combined. And for John, truly "to know" Jesus
is to believe. Jesus asks me at times, as he asked Philip (John 14:9), "Have
I been with you all this time, and you still do not know me?" And he asks
us, as he asked the disciples (16:32), "Do you now believe?" Despite their
assurances that yes, now they had really come to believe, Jesus tells them
that they will abandon him and then urges them to take courage, for the
Father is with him, and ultimately *in him* they may have peace. His faithfulness in the face of their wavering! And ours? And mine?

The Faith of Peter and Thomas

Peter, for all his warm, impulsive protestations of faith, has a long,
hard journey to real faith. He is the one who professed, "You are the Messiah, the Son of the Living God," apparently speaking out before any of
the other disciples. But shortly after, he protests that the suffering and
death Jesus predicts for himself must never happen. And he earns a sharp
rebuke for that lack of faith. "Get behind me Satan!" At the Last Supper
Peter says he would go to prison or death for Jesus—and within a very
short time he denies even knowing him. The tragic irony is heightened by
Jesus saying to Peter at the Supper, "Simon, Simon, . . . I have prayed for
you that your own faith may not fail; and you, when once you have turned
back, strengthen your brothers" (Luke 22:31-32). Almost immediately
Peter goes out and in weakness denies that he ever knew the man. It isn't
to the high priest that he makes the denial. It isn't anyone in a position

to overpower Peter, but a serving girl . . . and Peter's faith is not strong enough to stand before that kind of challenge. For all my protestations, am I so certain that my faith would stand?

After the Resurrection Jesus meets the apostles and, finally, Thomas with them. In response to Thomas's doubt, Jesus invites him to look at his pierced hands and feet, to put his fingers into the wound in his side, and to believe. And Thomas makes his great personal act of faith: "My Lord and my God!" Then Jesus again poses a challenge, "Have you believed because you have seen me? Blessed are those who have not seen and yet have come to believe" (John 20:25-29). This a blessing on followers of Jesus in every generation, including our own.

Our Faith and Trust in God

To the disciples on the way to Emmaus, disheartened, downhearted, apparently without real hope, Jesus says, "How slow of heart [you are] to believe" (Luke 24:25). How slow of heart—believing is a reality rooted in the heart, in that center of our being, of our personhood. All through the gospels it is as if Jesus has endlessly to urge and encourage—to hearten—and then persuade his followers to accept the gift that could bring them to life, full life, the life of faith.

Jesus has to deal with us similarly. We need to say with the father of the epileptic boy in Mark (9:24), "I believe; help my unbelief!" Jesus did not reject the father, and he healed his son. He did not reject the "slow of heart" in his own time and does not reject me or refuse to help my unbelief when I ask. The virtue of trust is intimately associated with faith. Perhaps what may hold us back from the real commitment to Jesus, and to his Father and their Spirit, is our inability or our hesitancy to really trust. Trust may be the gift God wishes to give me if I ask for it from the heart and then strive faithfully to exercise it.

The trust embedded in true faith frees us from fear and gives us the courage of a real disciple. "Do not fear!" recurs all through Scripture—over 350 times. There is a legitimate, necessary fear, and it, too, occurs frequently—"the fear of the Lord"—fear in the sense of profound awe, awareness of mystery, recognition of one's own unworthiness before the holiness of God. "The fear of the LORD is the beginning of wisdom" (Psalm 111:10; Proverbs 9:10); "The fear of the LORD is a fountain of life" (Proverbs 14:27); "Who among you fears the LORD and obeys the voice of his servant, who walks in darkness and has no light, yet trusts in the name of the LORD and relies upon his God?" (Isaiah 50:10).

It is not this fear that faith and trust overcome, but the complex of other fears that we are prone to. In a time of great fear among the people, Isaiah (35:4) exclaimed, "Be strong, do not fear! Here is your God. . . . He will come and save you." And again (43:1), "Do not fear, for I have redeemed you; I have called you by name, you are mine." The prophet Haggai (2:4-5, 19) urged, "I am with you . . . Do not fear . . . I will bless you." There is no promise that God will save us by removing the object of our fear. Rather, God's presence and our trust will strengthen us to overcome the fear, help us to place our energies where they belong—in trusting and in doing what we can—and then believing that God will see us through.

Courage

The opposite of fear is courage, and courage is rooted in faith. "Be strong! Let your heart take courage!" (Psalm 27:14). W. Paul Jones, a former United Methodist pastor ordained as a Catholic priest and an associate of a Cistercian monastery, describes courage as "faith's lifestyle"—a way to approach all of life. The apostle Paul gives this courage typical expression in 2 Corinthians (4:8-9), written late in his life, when he had been through a lot—so his words do not just express youthful verve and idealism, but represent tried virtue: "We are afflicted in every way, but not crushed; perplexed, but not driven to despair; persecuted, but not forsaken; struck down, but not destroyed; always carrying in the body the death of Jesus, so that the life of Jesus may also be made visible in our bodies." A little later (4:16) he continues: "So we do not lose heart. Even though our outer nature is wasting away, our inner nature is being renewed day by day." *There* is a life of courage, of trust, of faith!

We may all expect to be challenged in faith, trust, courage, sometimes severely. Then we need to make the necessary decisions from the center of our being, our heart where the Holy Spirit, the spirit of wisdom, resides.

And if we are to address that Spirit freely, we need to nourish by prayer the gifts of faith, trust, and courage as Thomas Merton did:

> My Lord God, I have no idea where I am going. I do not see the road ahead of me. I cannot know for certain where it will end. Nor do I really know myself, and the fact that I think I am following your will does not mean that I am actually doing so. But I believe that the desire to please you does in fact please you. And I hope I have that desire in all that I am doing. I hope that I will never do anything apart from that desire. And I know that if I do this you will lead me by the right road, though I may know nothing about it. Therefore I will trust you always though I may seem to be lost and in the shadow of death. I will not fear, for you are ever with me, and you will never leave me to face my perils alone.

Why do so many people today find faith and trust so difficult? Could the reason be our demand to understand? Is it mastery versus mystery? The ancient Greek translation of the Old Testament has Isaiah say, "Unless you believe, you will not understand." Sometimes we may want to invert this—"I cannot believe unless I understand." And this always brings to my mind Bonhoeffer's insight noted earlier, that unless you obey, you cannot believe. Together Isaiah and Bonhoeffer say: unless you obey, you cannot believe, and unless you believe, you cannot understand. In the eleventh century Saint Anselm echoed Isaiah: "I do not seek to understand that I may believe, but I believe in order to understand. For this also I believe— that unless I believe, I should not understand."

This is not to disparage the human search for knowledge. Surely many people who have spent long years in that search without having the gift of faith are brought to the point where they simply, humbly say, "This is beyond me." And however they understand the mystery, they bow to it. Does God not accept this?

I must treasure the gift of faith, nurture and deepen and exercise it in my daily life—not only for my own benefit surely, but for life in the Body of Christ. I am a member of that Body, and as I exercise the gifts God gives me, the Body of Christ is strengthened, to the blessing of the entire world.

Chapter 15

Can You Drink This Cup?

ESUS PUTS THE QUESTION TO EACH OF US TODAY as he did to James and John on the way to Jerusalem, the place where he had just predicted for the third time that he would suffer, die, and be raised to life: "Are you able to drink the cup that I am about to drink?" (Matthew 20:22).

At the heart of the gospel and of our Christian discipleship is the paschal mystery—dying in order to live, to live with that abundance, that fullness of life for which Christ utterly gave himself. Because it is so central to Christian faith and yet challenges that faith so deeply, Jesus repeatedly raises the question about suffering, dying, and rising.

Luke (24:13-35) tells us that Jesus was with two disciples on the road to Emmaus after his Resurrection, and they were lamenting the death of the one who, they said, they had hoped was the one to redeem Israel. Jesus finally broke through their dejection and incomprehension by breaking for them both word and bread, so that they knew he was indeed alive. Then, having chided them about their slowness to believe all that the prophets had foretold about the Messiah, he put the question to them: "Was it not necessary that the Messiah should suffer these things and then enter into his glory?" (Luke 24:26).

157

This question echoes three events that triggered Jesus' prediction of this central mystery of his life and of his disciples' faith—predictions that came at Peter's confession of faith at Caesarea Philippi (Matthew 16; Mark 8; Luke 9), Jesus' healing an epileptic boy whom the disciples could not heal (Matthew 17; Mark 9; Luke 9), and the story of the rich young man who could not bring himself to pay the cost of discipleship (Matthew 19-20; Mark 10; Luke 18).

Christ's Suffering, Dying, and Rising

At the first prediction of the passion, just after he recognized Jesus as the Messiah, Son of the living God, Peter (as Matthew and Mark have it) began to rebuke Jesus, saying, "God forbid it, Lord! This must never happen to you." And Jesus rebuked Peter for judging by human standards instead of God's. At the second prediction, the first three gospel writers say that the disciples were deeply distressed—they didn't understand at all, and were afraid to question the Lord. Perhaps like us, they hesitated to ask questions at this critical time because they were afraid there would only be confirmation of what they feared. And after the third and more detailed prediction of the imminent passion, only Luke remarks explicitly that the disciples didn't understand. However, all three evangelists proceed immediately to describe the disciples' dispute about who was to be the greatest. Their total incomprehension was all too evident.

Would we do better? Given our faith now, can we be sure we would comprehend, or even want to comprehend, that he for whom we had left everything that was or seemed to be familiar and secure in life, he who had given such evidence of authority and power, he whom we had recognized as the anointed Son of the living God, especially he whose way we were committed to follow—could we comprehend and accept that *he* would come to this?

Between the first and second prediction, Jesus asked the disciples why Scripture says that the Son of Man must "go through many sufferings and be treated with contempt" (Mark 9:12). And indeed it is evident in the gospels that he did suffer much and was despised and held in contempt long before the passion itself. Shortly after Jesus had chosen the Twelve, so great a crowd gathered about him that Mark (3:20-21) says Jesus and the Twelve could not even get time to eat, and his family came to take charge of him because "people were saying, 'He has gone out of his mind.'" John (7:5) writes in the same vein: "Not even his brothers believed in him."

We know he was rejected in his own town where surface familiarity kept people from any real insight into his character, his gifts, to say nothing of his vocation, his place in their sacred history. Their lack of faith thwarted his healing ministry so that he could do no more healing there. "And," writes Mark (6:6), "he was amazed at their unbelief."

And so the story continued. Reading between the lines throughout his public life, before that final Passover, we can know something of the pain he experienced: incomprehension, misunderstanding, attribution of wrong motives for his deeds, rejection, human aloneness even when he was in the midst of those closest to him, growing awareness of where his own fidelity was leading him. Jesus had devoted himself to teaching and forming his disciples, and he really could not count on them. John says that when Jesus taught the people about the Bread of Life, many of the disciples left him, and we can almost hear the pain in his voice when he asked the Twelve (6:67): "Do you also wish to go away?"

At the time of his arrest, after one of his chosen had betrayed him with the sign of friendship (Mark 14:44), when the volatile Peter cut off the ear of Malchus, the high priest's slave (John 18:10), Jesus deplored such response of violence to violence. Though the victim of violence himself, he never exercised violence in return. We remember that at the testing in the desert before Jesus began his public ministry, Satan challenged him to throw himself down from the pinnacle of the temple and trust that God would, as Psalm 91 promised, command angels to bear him up unharmed. Jesus, in turn, challenged Satan in the words of Deuteronomy, and Satan left. Angels did then, the gospels tell us, come to minister to him. Luke concludes his account of the temptation in the desert by saying Satan left Jesus "until an opportune time" (Luke 4:13).

This now, the anguish in Gethsemane, is that opportune time. Jesus faces "the cup" of suffering and death and knows his Father asks him to accept it. He asks to be spared but seeks even more deeply to do God's will. So Jesus could tell Peter to put back his sword and tell Judas and the crowd: "Do you think that I cannot appeal to my Father, and he will at once send me more than twelve legions of angels? But," he adds, "how then would the scriptures be fulfilled, which say it must happen this way?" (Matthew 26:53-54).

And so Jesus goes through that awful sequence of pain and mockery and abandonment, to his death.

Participation in the Suffering of Jesus

Have we put ourselves in Jesus' place through all this, not merely sentimentally, but really? Unless we do, can we truly accept our participation as disciples in his suffering? For participate we must if we would really follow him. Jesus asks us as he asked the chosen among his disciples, "Are you able to drink the cup that I am about to drink?" (Matthew 20:22).

The phrase has a long history and really means: "Can I accept my destiny?" For Jesus it meant, "Can I do this that my Father asks? Can I willingly take on this role and all its demands?" These questions become our questions. All too characteristically we, God's chosen ones, answer with an immediate, "We can." And Jesus tells us simply, "You shall!"

Perhaps I, too, say with good will but a little too impulsively, "I can!" And perhaps I speak too easily of the paschal mystery and my participation in it, and find out in pain and dismay how deep a mystery it really is. We want to follow Christ, but we never dreamed it would be like this! But if I really am to participate, I have to enter his temptations in my desert, my Gethsemane, my darkness, my weakness and powerlessness, finally in my death. And we must die, not only as he died, but again as the whole New Testament tells us, in his death. And really die.

If Jesus said of himself (Luke 24: 26), "Was it not necessary that the Messiah should suffer these things and then enter into his glory?"—and if we want to return to the Father in Christ, to that fullness of life that is glory—do we not have to undergo "all this"? If we say with Peter, "God forbid!" do we not have to expect the response that Peter got for judging God's will by human standards? Jesus has said plainly, "If any want to become my followers, let them deny themselves and take up their cross daily and follow me" (Luke 9:23). In taking up our cross daily, not as we choose it but as it is given, we drink the cup with him, the cup of pain that becomes the cup of salvation. And in those awesome words of Paul, "in my flesh I am completing what is lacking in Christ's afflictions for the sake of his body, that is, the church" (Colossians 1:24).

Reclaiming the Paschal Mystery

But as surely as we recognize that the paschal mystery—and our own paschal journey—involves dying, just so surely must we recognize that it is not a matter of dying only, even in the obedience of love. Suffering isn't enough. Dying isn't enough. If it were, we would then be, in the words of Paul, "of all people most to be pitied" (1 Corinthians 15:19). The finality is rising out of that death into newness of life, life beyond our present capacity to comprehend. Otherwise, as Jesus asked his disciples at the Last Supper, "Would I have told you that I go to prepare a place for you?" (John 14:2).

For most of us, I expect, the dying is all too experiential—the daily dying as well as the ultimate dying to earthly life. The rising, again both the daily and the ultimate, we take on faith; but when we really believe, there is joy. That whole cloud of witnesses, of which Hebrews 11 speaks, is there to encourage us, to assure us, to share their own joy.

And there are such witnesses in our own day, witnesses to the kind of life we can live even now if we enter freely and lovingly into the dying and rising of Christ. The paschal mystery that Mother Teresa lived in both its facets—the dying and the rising—was written in her face. Years ago she wrote to me: "Jesus has taken everything." A complete emptying, a willing emptying, even a joyful one. And consequently the transformation of so many lives! We all can recount the names and lives of others of the great cloud of witnesses throughout history and in our own era.

If we are attentive we see that every community, monastic or otherwise, has members who enter deeply into the paschal mystery—both the pain of dying and the joy of rising. But all too often we don't notice them. I think we may be doing what the people of Nazareth did. We are sure we know the person, have known him or her for years, have noted all their idiosyncrasies and many of their mistakes—but often do not really

When I was about nine my cousin and I were walking in the fields near the cemetery in Foley where my mother had been buried when I was six months old. The snow was a brilliant white in the winter sun. Someone had shot a male Chinese pheasant and left it lying in the snow. I can still see the intensity of color in its feathers and the drops of its life blood against the purity of the snow. I don't remember thinking or saying anything.

When I was in eighth grade my "second mother" (who was also my mother's sister and my godmother) was suddenly critically ill. I was home alone. I remember walking up to the hospital that spring evening, intensely conscious of the vibrancy of life all around me—the air, the color, the sounds, the intensity of a familiar world coming to life. I knew that this clarity of perception of life was related to my fear of death.

Later, as these two memories associated with each other, they became intimate symbols of death-and-life, too deep, too close to the center for analyzing, dismantling, reconnecting. They simply are.

—*Grace Notes*

recognize the depth of their lives. We may recognize them when they are old; we may not really know them until they have died. It has been a special joy to me in my own community, in recent years, when some unassuming, quietly dedicated community member whom we may not have really known fills the chapel to overflowing for her wake and funeral Mass—people who speak gratefully of her faith, her compassion, her patience in illness, her warmth, her humor, her service.

We are blessed to live in an age in the church that has reclaimed theologically and liturgically, and continues to do so pastorally, the richness of the paschal mystery and its implications for our Christian life. I remember that as a child I attended a seemingly endless number of daily "black Masses" and sang an abundance of *Dies Iraes* ("Day of Wrath") in the children's choir. The Second Vatican Council restored the wholeness of the mystery. The paschal mystery is one mystery, and we need to recognize and celebrate both aspects, death and resurrection, in their completeness and their relatedness. To do this, and to help others bring it to realization in their lives, we have to internalize it by the grace of God very deeply ourselves. The cup of suffering becomes the cup of salvation.

Chapter 16

Do You Love Me?

HE QUESTION THE LORD ASKS US NOW is one reported at the end of John's Gospel, part of the last recorded discussion with a number of his disciples on the shore of the Sea of Tiberias. And it will be the final, the definitive question asked again of each of us in our last hour: "Do you love me?" (John 21:15-17).

The Definitive Question of Peter

The occasion was the third of Jesus' post-resurrection appearances recounted by John. When Peter announced to his companions that he was going fishing, a number of others joined him. Their efforts all through the night were fruitless, but in the early morning light Jesus greeted them from the shore, and directed them to a remarkable catch of fish before they recognized him. He had prepared a breakfast for them, giving them bread and fish. After breakfast Jesus asked Peter three times: "Simon son of John, do you love me?"

Transformed and empowered now in resurrection faith, Peter could respond, "Yes, Lord; you know that I love you." Each time Jesus charged him with a shepherd's responsibility, and then said, "Follow me"—that is, follow my way as good shepherd of my sheep, and follow me in the ultimate self-giving this vocation will demand of you (John 21:15-19).

Earlier, during the Last Supper, Jesus had told the disciples that he was going to leave them and they couldn't follow him. Peter asked boldly, "Why can I not follow you now? I will lay down my life for you." And Jesus responded that Peter would in fact very soon deny him three times (John 13:36-38).

Now, after the Resurrection, the compassionate Jesus gives Peter the gift of a triple assertion of a love purified, matured, and deepened with tears of compunction. And now Jesus invites, calls Peter to follow him—something Peter can now do because he is humbled, transformed, graced. Now he would be called to lay down his life for his friend and Lord.

Jesus asks not only Peter, but each of us today: "Do you love me?" We cannot answer unless we dwell in his love for us, for that is the only way we can come to know what true love means. Jesus is love and the source of all love. We can love, we have love, only in his love.

Jesus' love, believed in, known, experienced, makes it possible for us to love—with love that is not just an imitation. The reality and experience of being loved as Jesus loves opens up our capacity to participate in his love (1 John 4:15-16). So we have known and believe the love God has for us.

God's Everlasting, Steadfast, Faithful Love

From the beginning to the end, Scripture speaks of the character, the characteristics of divine love. God's love is endlessly enduring, *everlasting*. The psalmist picks this up from countless texts such as Jeremiah 31:3: "I have loved you with an everlasting love." The refrain in Psalm 136 says, ". . . his steadfast love endures forever." God's love is constant, dependable, *steadfast*, and is frequently linked with "everlasting." Even in his anguish over the mystery of the suffering of the innocent, Job (10:12) prayed, "You have granted me life and steadfast love." And God's love is *faithful*, is firm and undeviating. "Know therefore that the LORD your God is God, the faithful God who maintains covenant loyalty with those who love him and keep his commandments" (Deuteronomy 7:9).

These three defining qualities of God's love are drawn together in Isaiah (54:8, 10): "With everlasting love I will have compassion on you, says the LORD your Redeemer. . . . For the mountains may depart and the hills be removed, but my steadfast love shall not depart from you, and my covenant of peace shall not be removed." This is surely a promise of love. God promised a new covenant and the gift of new hearts that we might truly love. And God would send the Son and Spirit to indwell these hearts, so that Love itself would indwell us.

God so loved the world that God sent the only Son, the Beloved, so that we might have life, and have it abundantly (John 3:16; 10:10). Jesus, then, incarnated God's love, God's life-giving love, God's compassionate love. Jesus lived his life for love and at the end gave over his life for love. His words communicate love, invite love. Jesus said, "As the Father has loved me, so I have loved you" (John 15:9). This love asks two things: that we truly hear his word and that we keep his commandments. And those commandments are to love, to love God in Christ's own love, and to love one another as Christ has loved us. At his death he gave over his Spirit of love whom he had promised at the Supper, another Advocate in whom Jesus would be with us forever.

We love only because God first loved us (1 John 4:19). In Saint Bernard's words, "Man loves indeed, but not without reason, for he knows that he is loved without desert; he loves without end because he knows that he was loved before the beginning of time." William Blake has a famous and lovely line about God's love:

> We are put on this earth a little space
> That we may learn to bear the beams of love.

And Thérèse of Lisieux, in her autobiography concluded: "Love, in fact, is the vocation that includes all others."

Desire Urges Us to Seek God's Love

This is the incomprehensible mystery, that God desires our love. God who is love desires to be loved by us. God wants us to know God in loving God—the knowing that comes only from loving. When Jesus asked Peter if he loved him, Peter could then respond (John 21:17), "Lord, you know everything; you know that I love you," because Peter now knew so deeply and so humbly that Jesus loved him. To love is to serve as Jesus. The self-emptying servant taught and demonstrated this in his own life, and immediately directed Peter to service: "Feed my lambs . . . Tend my sheep . . . Feed my sheep" (21:15-17). And we are called to do no less, to love and serve as Jesus did.

So now Jesus asks us, each of us: "Do you love me?" How do we meet Jesus' criteria for loving him? Do we really hear and believe Jesus' word and keep his commandments? We may well discover that this question about loving Jesus recapitulates all the questions we have been reflecting on because they are all measures of our love for Jesus. Where am I? What am I looking for? Who do I say that you are? With what do I come before you in worship and prayer? Where and how real is my faith? Can I drink the cup of suffering that Jesus drank?

We might have to answer these questions with some hesitation. However, knowing something of Jesus' measureless and patient love that makes love possible in us, we can say honestly and humbly, "Yes, Lord, you know that I love you."

But we long to love Jesus more, more steadfastly, more deeply, more faithfully. And when we understand from the Scriptures and from the lives of that great cloud of witnesses just how pervasive and effective desire is, we can be at peace and answer, "Yes, Lord." Desire urges us to seek, and God has promised from the beginning to the end of Scripture, "You will seek the LORD your God, and you will find him if you search after him with all your heart and soul" (Deuteronomy 4:29).

The same consoling and challenging message recurs all through the living tradition. Saint Augustine stated repeatedly that the very desire to pray is prayer. Is not then the desire to love in fact love? Saint Benedict makes it clear in his Rule that the monastic life is for people of desire, and that the life is meant to cultivate and deepen desire.

Suffering Nourishes a Desire for God's Love

Times of struggle, confusion, and suffering nourish in many a deepened desire for God. This surely applies to the fourteenth century. The

FIRE ON THE EARTH! KINDLE LOVE IN MY SOUL!

*I*f no more, then a small flame, enclosed but undying,
Its white heat of fire pointing upward and trying
To burn, to make futile the darkening, to light
The image of you through the night
Of the purging—a small flame to love's conflagration
     replying.

—*Grace Notes*

great witnesses of that time have a special appeal for many today. It has been called "the terrible century" with the ravages of the bubonic plague that reduced populations by half in some parts of Europe, the Hundred Years War, the time of the Avignon Papacy, poverty, misery, disease, divisions of every sort. It became a century of great saints, great spiritual literature, and great spiritual movements.

Catherine of Siena's *Dialogue* is almost marinated in desire. She has God say, "I am not a respecter of persons or status but of holy desires." And, "I am the one who answers holy longings." An older translation has Catherine say, "God does not ask a perfect work but infinite desire." And God the Father speaks to Catherine of his being bound by the chains of her desire for reform in the church. If Gregory the Great had not been called the Doctor of Desire, the title might well go to Catherine.

Another testament to desire in Catherine's century is the unknown author of *The Cloud of Unknowing*. I cited him earlier, but he bears frequent repetition. He speaks again and again of "a naked intent toward God." He begins the work by insisting, "If you wish to keep growing you must nourish in your heart the lively longing for God. Though this loving desire is certainly God's gift, it is up to you to nurture it." And recall that he ends, "It is not what you are nor what you have been that God sees with his all-merciful eyes, but what you desire to be."

And Julian of Norwich, virtually forgotten for so long a time and now so important to many, speaks of God's longing for us and his word to her: "I am who makes you to love, I am who makes you to long, I it am, the endless fulfilling of all true desires." In the midst of her own suffering and the sufferings of her century she heard Jesus say to her, "all shall be well. And all shall be well. And all manner of thing shall be well."

The Definitive Question for Us

So, Lord—you ask if we love you. Trusting in your word to those who loved you, trusting in your love that makes ours possible and capable of endless deepening, endless growth in fidelity—Yes, Lord, you know that we love you with at least the beginning of such love, and we know that it is your gift. We ask that you increase our love, deepen our love so that we truly seek you, truly love your word and want to live by it, truly love the life-giving, healing, and nurturing of your sacraments, truly love and seek to do your will, truly and lovingly serve our neighbor in our love for you as your Spirit directs.

Do I love you? Yes, Lord. Increase my love.

Acknowledgments

*T*HIS BOOK GREW OUT OF REQUESTS for retreats for monastic communities, generous encouragement from many participants, and the invaluable assistance of competent and dedicated supporters.

My debt to Saint Benedict's Monastery and its prioress, Sister Nancy Bauer, OSB, and to Mr. Peter Dwyer, Director of the Liturgical Press, is immense. Mr. Dwyer has been a consistent observer, supporter, and evaluator in the process of bringing the work to press.

Dr. Patrick Henry's editing out of a rich theological background unfailingly improved the text; his indispensable enthusiasm and his insights frequently enriched the content. Kathleen Kalinowski, OSB, dedicated the time and effort to type the text and provided much of the impetus for discussions, evaluations, and improvements. Stefanie Weisgram, OSB, librarian at the College of Saint Benedict and Saint John's University, in addition to supplying documentary services, contributed to ongoing decisiveness and recommendations.

I am also most grateful to Kathleen Norris, who volunteered to write the foreword to this book.

Without the sustained interest and support from these people, this book would not have come to be. My gratitude is deep and abiding.

Jeremy Hall, OSB

References

Excerpts from the Rule are from *RB 1980: The Rule of Benedict in English*, ed. by Timothy Fry, OSB (Collegeville, MN: The Liturgical Press, 1982).

Excerpts from *Sayings of the Desert Fathers: The Alphabetical Collection*, trans. by Benedicta Ward, SLG, Cistercian Studies 59 (Kalamazoo, MI: Cistercian Publications, 1975), are quoted by permission of Benedicta Ward, SLG.

Excerpts from *The Desert Fathers*, trans. by Helen Waddell (London: Constable & Co Ltd, 1987 [1936]), are quoted by permission of Constable & Robinson Ltd, London, and The University of Michigan Press, Ann Arbor.

page

vii   Auden: "For the Time Being: A Christmas Oratorio," section "The Flight into Egypt, IV," in Marvin Halverson, ed., *Religious Drama 1*, originally published 1945 by Random House (New York: Living Age Books, 1957) 68.

3   G. K. Chesterton: "Homesick at Home," in *Daylight and Nightmare: Uncollected Stories and Fables*, selected by Marie Smith (New York: Dodd, Mead & Company, 1986) 24–27.

6   Abba Lot: *Sayings of the Desert Fathers: The Alphabetical Collection*, trans. by Benedicta Ward, SLG, Cistercian Studies 59 (Kalamazoo, MI: Cistercian Publications, 1975) 103 (#7).

page

Gregory of Nyssa: *The Life of Moses*, trans. by Abraham J. Malherbe and Everett Ferguson, Classics of Western Spirituality, Cistercian Studies 31 (New York: Paulist Press, 1978) 114–16 (#232, 233, 239).

8   Dostoevsky: *The Brothers Karamazov*, trans. by Richard Pevear and Larissa Volokhonsky (New York: Vintage Books, 1991) 164.

8–9   Gregory of Nyssa: *On the Song of Songs*, 11, 12, cited by Malherbe and Ferguson, *The Life of Moses*, "Introduction," 21–22.

9   Mother Teresa: *A Gift for God: Prayers and Meditations* (San Francisco: Harper & Row, 1975) 17.

      Among Desert Fathers: "The Sayings of the Fathers," in *The Desert Fathers*, trans. by Helen Waddell (London: Constable & Co Ltd, 1987 [1936]) 7.38, 128.

      Julian of Norwich: *Showing of Love*, trans. by Julia Bolton Holloway (Collegeville, MN: The Liturgical Press, 2003) ch. 10, 18.

12   Thomas à Kempis: *Imitation of Christ*, trans. by Ronald Knox and Michael Oakley (New York: Sheed and Ward, 1959) 2.1, 62.

      MacDonald: *Lilith*, ch. 31, in *Phantastes and Lilith* (Grand Rapids, MI: Wm. B. Eerdmans Publishing Company, 1964 [1895]) 331.

13   Gregory the Great: *Dialogues*, trans. by Odo John Zimmerman, OSB, Fathers of the Church 39 (New York: Fathers of the Church, Inc., 1959) 2.3, 62.

14   *Dialogues* 2.35, 104–05.

19   Brother Roger: "Taizé: Continuity and the Provisional," *Monastic Studies* 4 (1966) 91.

20–22 Ward: *Sayings*, 234 (Syncletica #16); 239 (Hyperechius #8); 196 (Pambo #3).

23   Brother Roger: *Parable of Community: The Rule and Other Basic Texts of Taizé* (New York: The Seabury Press, 1981) 34.

24   Kierkegaard: *Søren Kierkegaard's Journals and Papers*, ed. and trans. by Howard V. Hong and Edna H. Hong, vol. 1 (Bloomington: Indiana University Press, 1967) #936 (from the year 1846) 411; vol. 2 (1970) #1255 (from the year 1848) 64.

page

Augustine: *The Free Choice of the Will*, trans. by Robert P. Russell, OSA, Fathers of the Church 59 (Washington, DC: The Catholic University of America Press, 1968) 2.2.6, 112–13. Augustine is here dependent on the ancient Greek (Septuagint) translation of Isaiah 7:9.

Bonhoeffer: *The Cost of Discipleship*, rev. ed. (New York: The Macmillan Company, 1959) 56–57.

Desert Fathers: Ward, *Sayings*, 154 (Nisterius #2).

Augustine: *Tractates on the First Epistle of John*, trans. by John W. Rettig, Fathers of the Church 92 (Washington, DC: The Catholic University of America Press, 1995) 7.8, 223.

25   *George MacDonald: An Anthology*, ed. by C. S. Lewis (New York: Macmillan, 1978) 142 (from *What's Mine's Mine*, ch. 15).

Leclercq: "Benedictine Freedom," *Cistercian Studies* 16 (1981) 273.

26   Merton: "The Monk Today," one of two appendices to ch. 13 of *Contemplation in a World of Action* (Garden City, NY: Doubleday & Company, Inc., 1971) 227. The two appendices are omitted in the 1998 reprint of the book (Notre Dame, IN: University of Notre Dame Press).

27   Leclercq: "Benedictine Freedom," 279.

28   Wathen: "The Word of Silence: On Silence and Speech in RB," *Cistercian Studies* 17 (1982) 200.

29   Undset: *Christmas and Twelfth Night* (New York: Longmans, Green & Co., 1932) 34–35.

Kierkegaard: *Training in Christianity and the Edifying Discourse which "accompanied" it*, trans. by Walter Lowrie (Princeton: Princeton University Press, 1960 [1941]) 190.

Desert Fathers: *The Wisdom of the Desert: Sayings from the Desert Fathers of the Fourth Century*, trans. by Thomas Merton (New York: New Directions, 1960) 47, 54.

Pachomius: *Pachomian Koinonia III: Instructions, Letters, and Other Writings of Saint Pachomius and His Disciples*, Cistercian Studies Series 47 (Kalamazoo, MI: Cistercian Publications, 1982) 35.

page

Dorotheus: "On the Structures and Harmony of the Virtues of the Soul," *Discourses and Sayings*, trans. by Eric P. Wheeler (Kalamazoo, MI: Cistercian Publications, 1977) 203.

31–32   Hume: "The Monastic Ideal in Earthenware Vessels," *American Benedictine Review* 32/1 (1981) 6–7.

32   *Book of Degrees*: Andre Louf, "The Word Beyond the Liturgy," *Cistercian Studies* 6 (1971) 360–64.

33   Ward: *Sayings*, 22 (Agathon #9); 56 (Epiphanius #3).

35   Theophan: *The Art of Prayer: An Orthodox Anthology*, compiled by Igumen Chariton of Valamo, trans. by E. Kadloubovsky and E. M. Palmer, ed. by Timothy Ware (London: Faber and Faber Limited, 1966) 53, 90.

MacDonald: *Anthology*, 128 (from *Thomas Wingfold, Curate*, ch. 74).

Spurgeon: *The Treasury of David: containing an Original Exposition of the Book of Psalms; a Collection of Illustrative Extracts from the whole range of literature; a Series of Homiletical Hints upon almost every verse; and Lists of Writers upon each Psalm*, vol. 1 (London: Passmore & Alabaster, 1870; reproduced at Pasadena, TX: Pilgrim Publications, 1983) 50 (on Psalm 5:3).

36   Pachomius: *Pachomian Koinonia II: Pachomian Chronicles and Rules*, Cistercian Studies Series 46 (Kalamazoo, MI: Cistercian Publications, 1981) 16, 156, 202.

Guigo II: *The Ladder of Monks and Twelve Meditations*, trans. by Edmund Colledge, OSA, and James Walsh, SJ (Garden City, NY: Image Books, 1978).

John of the Cross: *The Collected Works of St. John of the Cross*, trans. by Kieran Kavanaugh, OCD, and Otilio Rodriguez, OCD (Washington, DC: ICS Publications, 1978) "Maxims and Counsels" #79, 680.

37   Koch: Quoted by Fidelis Ruppert, OSB, "Meditatio – Ruminatio: Zu einem Grundbegriff christlicher Meditation," *Erbe und Auftrag* 53 (1977) 93; French translation, "Meditatio – Ruminatio: Une méthode traditionnelle de méditation," *Collectanea Cisterciensia* 39/1 (1977) 92–93.

page

38   William of St. Thierry: *The Golden Epistle*, trans. by Theodore
          Berkeley, OCSO, Cistercian Fathers Series 12 (Spencer, MA:
          Cistercian Publications, 1971) 1.31, 51–52.

38–39   Guigo: 86–87 (*Ladder*, chs. 6 and 7); 134 (*Meditations*, ch. 10).

41   Casey: "Mindfulness of God in the Monastic Tradition," *Cister-
          cian Studies* 17/2 (1982) 123.

42   Ward: *Sayings*, 120–21 (Lucius #1).

43   Ward: *Sayings*, 76 (Theodore #16).
          Serapion: "History of the Monks of Egypt," in Waddell, *Desert
          Fathers*, 17, 73–74.

45   Catherine of Siena: *The Dialogue*, trans. by Suzanne Noffke, OP,
          Classics of Western Spirituality (New York: Paulist Press, 1980)
          ch. 7, 36.
          Mother Teresa: *A Gift for God*, 76.

46   Demetrius Dumm: "Benedictine Hospitality," *Benedictines* 35/2
          (Fall–Winter 1980) 64–75.

46–47   Cassian: "The Sayings of the Fathers," in Waddell, *Desert Fathers*,
          13.2, 160.

47   Easter: *Dialogues* 2.1, 58–59.

48   Newman: "The Mission of St. Benedict," originally published
          in *Atlantis* (January 1858), in *Essays and Sketches*, vol. 3, ed.
          by Charles Frederick Harrold (New York: Longmans, Green &
          Co., 1948) 235–92.
          Dubos: "Franciscan Conservation versus Benedictine Steward-
          ship," in *A God Within* (New York: Charles Scribner's Sons, 1972)
          153–74.

49   Muir: *The Yosemite* (New York: The Century Co., 1920) 28.

49–50   Aelred: Walter Daniel, *The Life of Aelred of Rievaulx*, trans. by
          F. M. Powicke, Cistercian Fathers Series 5 (Kalamazoo, MI: Cis-
          tercian Publications, 1994) ch. 29, 117–18.

50   Ward: "Introduction," *The Lives of the Desert Fathers: The Historia
          Monachorum in Aegypto*, trans. by Norman Russell, Cistercian Stud-
          ies Series 34 (Kalamazoo, MI: Cistercian Publications, 1981) 34.
          Ward: *Sayings*, 225 (Sarmatas #1).

page

52   Gregory: *Dialogues*, 3.34, 173–74.
          Ward: *Sayings*, 138–39 (Moses #2); 134 (Macarius #32).

52–53   Ward, *Sayings*, 96 (Isidore #1).

53   Ward: *Sayings*, 214 (Sisoes #12).

54   Augustine: *Sermon 88*, in *Sermons III (51–94) on the New Testament*, trans. by Edmund Hill, OP, The Works of Saint Augustine: A Translation for the 21st Century (Brooklyn, NY: New City Press, 1991) 5, 422.
          Pachomius: *Pachomian Koinonia I: The Life of Saint Pachomius and His Disciples*, Cistercian Studies Series 45 (Kalamazoo, MI: Cistercian Publications, 1980) 69.

54–55   Manufactured quarrel: *Wisdom of the Desert*, 67.

55   Merton: *Conjectures of a Guilty Bystander* (Garden City, NY: Doubleday & Company, 1966) 73.

60   Edward Abbey: *Desert Solitaire* (Tucson: The University of Arizona Press, 1988) 227–28.

70   Eucherius: "In Praise of the Desert," *Cistercian Studies* 11/1 (1976) 66.

74   Mother Teresa: *Words to Live By* (Notre Dame, IN: Ave Maria Press, 1983) 44.

77   Ignatius: *Letter to the Romans* 7:2, in *Early Christian Fathers*, trans. by Cyril C. Richardson, The Library of Christian Classics, vol. 1 (London: SCM Press Ltd, 1953) 105.
          John of the Cross: *Collected Works*, "Maxims and Counsels" #21, 675.

78   Hammarskjöld: *Markings* (New York: Alfred A. Knopf, 1965) 39.

78–79   Buechner: *The Sacred Journey* (San Francisco: Harper & Row, Publishers, 1982) 103.

79–80   *The Journal of John Woolman and a Plea for the Poor* (Secaucus, NJ: The Citadel Press, 1972) 11–12, 216.

80–83   Guitton: "Solitude and Silence," *Monastic Studies* 2 (1964) 49.

89   Nouwen: *The Way of the Heart* (New York: The Seabury Press, 1981) 40.
          Lindbergh: *Gift from the Sea* (New York: Pantheon, 1975) 52–53.

page

91   Rilke: *Letters to a Young Poet*, trans. by Stephen Mitchell (New
          York: Random House, 1984) 78.
          Augustine: *Confessions*, trans. by Henry Chadwick (Oxford: Ox-
          ford University Press, 1991) 3.6.11, 43.

94–95   Merton: "Notes for a Philosophy of Solitude," in *Disputed Ques-
          tions* (Farrar, Straus & Cudahy, 1960), 198; *A Vow of Conversation:
          Journals 1964–1965* (New York: Farrar•Straus•Giroux, 1988) 204.

96   Rule of hospitality: "The Sayings of the Fathers," in Waddell,
          Desert Fathers, 13.7, 160.
          Ammon: "History of the Monks of Egypt," in Waddell, *Desert
          Fathers*, 22, 77–78.

103   Gandhi: On Jesus: "What Jesus Means to Me," *Modern Review*,
          October 1941, in *The Collected Works of Mahatma Gandhi*, vol.
          75 (Ahmedabad, India: Navajivan Press, 1979) 69. On simplic-
          ity: "Position of Women," *Young India*, July 21, 1921, in *Collected
          Works*, vol. 20 (1966) 410.
          Graham: The Billy Graham Evangelistic Association is unable to
          confirm whether this was said by Graham, or, if he said it, whether
          it was original with him. Many Web sites attribute it to him, but
          others attribute it to "as the saying goes" or "as my mother told me"
          or "as a good friend reminded me once" or "as we say in Texas."
          The phrase is also the title and theme of several recorded songs.

105   Brother Roger: *A Life We Never Dared Hope For: Journals 1972–
          1974* (Nashville, TN: The Upper Room; New York: The Seabury
          Press, 1981) 31.

107–08   *Walden: or, Life in the Woods*, annotated by Bill McKibben (Bos-
          ton: Beacon Press, 1997 [1854]) chs.1 and 2, 64, 76, 85, 21, 12.

107   Woolman: *Journal*, 41–42.

108   Hammarskjöld: *Markings*, 91.

111   Rahner: Karl Rahner and Herbert Vorgrimler, *Theological Dic-
          tionary* (New York: Herder and Herder, 1965) 370.

112   Mother Teresa: *Words to Live By*, 42.

113   Temple: *Readings in St. John's Gospel (First and Second Series)*
          (London: Macmillan & Co Ltd, 1959 [1945]) 189–90.

114   Long, loving look at the real: attributed to William McNamara,
          OCD.

page

116   Bolt: *A Man for All Seasons: A Play in Two Acts* (New York: Vintage Books, 1962) Preface, xi.

117   O'Donovan: *Benedict of Nursia* (London: Collins, 1980) 5.

118   Merton: *Contemplative Prayer* (New York: Herder and Herder, 1969) 39, 82–83.

131–32 *The Cloud of Unknowing*, ed. by William Johnston (New York: Image Books, 1973) ch. 75, 134.

135–36 Merton: *The New Man* (New York: Farrar, Straus & Giroux, 1961) 43, 67.

136   Ruysbroeck: *De calculo* 8–9, quoted in Evelyn Underhill, *Mysticism: A Study in the Nature and Development of Man's Spiritual Consciousness*, 12th ed. (New York: E. P. Dutton and Company Inc., 1930) 433–34.

137   *Cloud of Unknowing*, ch. 2, 39.

140   Thomas Aquinas: *Exposition on John's Gospel*, 14.2, reading for Saturday of the ninth week in Ordinary Time, *Liturgy of the Hours According to the Roman Rite*, English translation prepared by the International Commission on English in the Liturgy (New York: Catholic Book Publishing Co., 1975) vol. 3, 315 16.

148   Torn cloak: *Wisdom of the Desert*, 76.

149   Ward: *Sayings*, 26 (Ammonas #3).

149–50 C. S. Lewis: *Letters*, ed. by W. H. Lewis (London: Bles, 1966) 230.

155   Jones: "Courage as the Heart of Faith," *Weavings* 12/3 (May/June 1997) 11.

156   Merton: *Thoughts in Solitude* (New York: Farrar, Straus & Cudahy, 1958) 83.

166   *The Letters of St Bernard of Clairvaux*, trans. by Bruno Scott James (Kalamazoo, MI: Cistercian Publications, 1998) 109.7, 162.
       Blake: "The Little Black Boy" (from *Songs of Innocence*, 1789).
       Thérèse: *The Story of a Soul*, ed. and trans. by Robert J. Edmonson (Brewster, MA: Paraclete Press, 2006) 217.

169   Catherine of Siena: *The Dialogue*, ch. 47, 97; ch. 51, 103.
       The Cloud of Unknowing: ch. 2, 47; ch. 75, 146.
       Julian: *Showing of Love*, ch. 59, 89; ch. 27, 37.

Glossary

Monastic terms

Abba and Amma: From the Aramaic, meaning "Father" and "Mother," terms applied to early monastic teachers, especially those associated with the Egyptian and Syrian deserts.

American Cassinese Congregation: A federation of twenty-one Benedictine men's monasteries that trace their lineage to the foundation of Saint Vincent's Archabbey in Latrobe, Pennsylvania, in 1846.

Cistercian: "Strict Observance" Benedictines, founded as a reform movement at the end of the eleventh century.

Coenobitic monasticism: The form of monastic life that is centered in community; the term comes from the Greek meaning "common life."

Eremitic monasticism (also called **Anchoritic**): The form of monastic life that is lived by individuals alone. The English term is hermit.

Monte Cassino: The principal Benedictine monastery, located between Rome and Naples, founded by Saint Benedict when he migrated from Subiaco about 529.

Opus Dei ("The Work of God"): The term used by Saint Benedict in the Rule to refer to the daily liturgy centered in the recitation of the Psalms. A common English term is the Daily Office.

Subiaco: The town forty miles east of Rome where Saint Benedict settled in a grotto to begin his monastic life.